THE
COMING COLLAPSE
OF THE
POST OFFICE

ROBERT J. MYERS

PRENTICE-HALL, INC.
Englewood Cliffs, New Jersey

The Coming Collapse of the Post Office, by Robert J. Myers

Copyright © 1975 by Robert J. Myers

Printed in the United States of America

Prentice-Hall International, Inc., London
Prentice-Hall of Australia, Pty. Ltd., Sydney
Prentice-Hall of Canada, Ltd., Toronto
Prentice-Hall of India Private Ltd., New Delhi
Prentice-Hall of Japan, Inc., Tokyo

10 9 8 7 6 5 4 3 2 1

Library of Congress Cataloging in Publication Data

Myers, Robert John.
    The coming collapse of the Post Office.

    1. United States Postal Service.   2. Postal
Service–United States.   I. Title.
HE6371.M93   383'.4'0973   75-5774
ISBN 0-13-152603-0

To my parents

INTRODUCTION

We Americans have a touching faith that all problems can be solved by our native genius for organization. What we have done in space we shall do in cancer research. Therefore, if our mail service is faulty, it must be because an organizational method went wrong. Some would conclude that if the vice is inefficiency, we should turn our mails over to the military (although evidence suggests that there never has been more waste and inefficiency than in the American Armed Forces). But in the case of the Postal Service, the actual prescription has been to remove the mails from government ineptitude and have the mail service run by businessmen, not strictly as a private enterprise, but as a government corporation. The prospective efficiencies were to keep postal rates low and service high.

Thus the present Postal Service came into being through the Postal Reorganization Act of 1970, the result of the recommendations of the Kappel Commission in 1968. These recommendations were not followed to the letter, but in general, they did provide for a radical reorganization of the old Post Office Department, going much further than many members of Congress wanted. The formula was to transform the Post Office from a traditional department of government into a government corporation along the administrative lines of the Tennessee Valley Authority. This would remove our mails from the pressures and evils of politics, enthusiasts claimed, and make the Post Office operate on a "hard-nosed" business basis. The impetus for this conversion was the wish to eliminate the perennial multimillion-dollar Post Office deficits and to solve the growingly insistent problems of how to manage the mails.

To date, the most obvious results of the reorganization have been a deterioration of the mail service and an increasingly expensive organization with rapidly expanding payrolls (about 85 percent of postal costs are now labor). A manpower year of labor now costs $14,100. By 1982, at present rates of pay increases, this figure will rise to $28,000 per man-year. The day of the twenty-cent first-class stamp is just over the next ridge.

Postal Service management suffers from fewer outside constraints than either public or private enterprise and enjoys higher salaries, more perquisites of office, and more fringe benefits. The several billions of dollars of public assets that were transferred from the Post Office to the new corporation are being used solely as the new managers see fit. True, there is sporadic congressional supervision in terms of long, loud, and inconclusive hearings. Yet as of this writing, the chairman of the Board of Governors has not seen the President of the United States, his actual boss, in over five years. The Board of Governors of the Postal Service and their chosen instrument, the Postmaster General, conduct this enormous business—now over $11 billion per year, the fourth largest corporation in America—solely as their personal judgment dictates.

The problem of handling the multitudinous affairs of the American Government is increasingly complex. Despite high taxes there are still not enough funds to go around. Deficits mount each year, and the public debt ceiling is raised annually. If an experiment on the scale of the Postal Service actually worked, it might set the trend for transferring to the private sector, or to the government corporation sector, other equally large areas of government operation. The chairman of the Board of Governors of the Postal Service has suggested this possibility in order to improve service, reduce costs, and remove the hand of government from more areas of our daily life.

There is certainly an argument for the private corporation approach instead of the government corporation, and this precedent may gain more credence and support unless the government corporation demonstrates impressive results. Alternatively, the whole affair could go full circle, back to the government, on the grounds that (as with the railroads) some vital areas of the economy must ultimately be managed by government. Indeed, that is why regulatory commissions have been set up to provide for an input of public interest to temper the naturally powerful inclination of monopoly interests in utilities or transportation to maximize profits at the expense of the taxpayers.

Since the passing of the Postal Reorganization Act in 1970 and the official formation of the Postal Service on July 1, 1971, there has been more than enough experience to indicate how well the reorganization is doing. Simply put, the results have been less for more—less service at much higher cost. This has affected, among other things, the traditional press freedoms of printed materials, based on low-cost access to the mails, and has called for new definitions of the public interest in postal matters. In the ongoing media and marketing revolutions, the costs of postal service may determine what areas will develop the fastest. The Postal Service appears to be headed toward the eye of a technological revolution in message moving that it is ill prepared to cope with.

INTRODUCTION

I admit to being more concerned about the Postal Service than many consumers are—yet. I am the publisher of a magazine with a small circulation. Monopoly government control of the mails, through the old Post Office or the new government corporation, constantly raises the prospect of regulation of the distribution of both newspapers and magazines. Even if such control did not result in direct censorship by a lawless government, it could produce a very effective kind of indirect censorship through service so poor that subscribers would be driven away or through mailing costs so high that publishing magazines would become prohibitively expensive for the publisher.

I began formally to carry out the research for this project in September 1972. I have attended or participated in most of the House and Senate hearings from 1969 through 1974. As a founder of the Committee for the Diversity of the Press in 1972, I have actively worked for special second-class postal rates for magazines with small circulations. During the past few years I have interviewed many officials of the Postal Service, from the chairman of the Board of Governors and the Postmaster General to my local letter carrier. Mrs. Isabelle Hall, formerly a special assistant to the Postmaster General for public relations, was particularly helpful in arranging for meetings with high-level postal officials. Beyond that, I owe a large debt of gratitude to many of the lawyers and lobbyists who represent the varied interests associated with the past and future of mail service in America. Errors of fact and judgment, however, are mine alone.

Robert J. Myers
Washington, D.C.

CONTENTS

I

CRACKS IN THE POST OFFICE

Did you attend the ceremonies at your local post office on July 1, 1971, when the changeover was made to the new government corporation, the United States Postal Service? Probably you weren't invited. You weren't asked whether you wanted this change from public service to private profit in the first place. Pity. Perhaps you would have said no.

Since then the men in light blue suits have become money changers, and the buildings themselves, temples to the gods of profit—not for the taxpayers, but for those who control and exploit the Postal Service for their own ends. The idea that the Postal Service is simply another monopoly public utility like the phone company was one of the contributions of the Kappel Commission, whose 1968 recommendations were the basis for the 1970 Reorganization Act. The implications of the "public utility" idea are now being made explicit as the Postal Service maps its fiscal program for the future. If ends and means don't meet, the Postal Service will simply apply for a rate increase, like the local gas or phone company. Four years ago the first-class stamp was six cents. As of this writing, it is ten cents, with nowhere to go but up.

The 1970 Reorganization Bill was passed in Congress over the objections of such critics as now retired Representative H. R. Gross (R., Iowa) and former Senator Ralph Yarborough (D., Texas). On June 30, 1970, in a pointed speech, Yarborough said: "The issue is plain and simple. Are we going to keep this branch of the U.S. Government for service, or are we going to turn it into a profit-motive thing that will subordinate service to profit?" This question continues to hang over the Postal Service's performance like a dark cloud.

What has been happening in the Postal Service since the 1970 reorganization would be laughable if it were not so damaging to the commercial and intellectual life of the country. In addition to setting the pattern for giant increases in federal salary costs (through ruinous postal union settlements), the postal system's record of declining service at higher costs has vast implications for our way of doing business, for the prospect of improving our quality of life, and even for the health of our democratic system. The trend of the times is toward monopoly, toward concentration of power, and of communications as an adjunct of that power. The Postal Reorganization Act, in its field, accelerates that trend. Its labor policies are feeding inflation and creating unmanageable payroll costs, which the sponsors of the reorganization unwittingly triggered when their cost formulas spread to the Defense Department and the rest of the federal bureaucracy. We have already priced ourselves out of a standing army, and perhaps someday the cost of the federal government itself may become equally prohibitive. Meantime as costs rise in the Postal Service, we can already witness a slowing down in the dissemination of ideas as more and more publications find they can no longer afford to distribute by mail.

Growing disenchantment with the fruits of the reorganization was widely expressed in the congressional hearings on the Postal Service in the spring of 1973, following the marked decline in service that began around Christmas 1972. During these hearings Senator Jennings Randolph (D., W. V.) cited a letter written in 1885 by the Trotter brothers of Staunton, Virginia. The brothers had a contract to move the mail from two rural areas. A heavy snowfall prevented them from crossing a particularly high mountain, and their customers complained. The Trotter brothers' response was this:

> Mr. Postmaster General
> Washington, D.C.
>
> Sir: If you knock the gable out of Hell and back it up against Cheat Mountain and rain fire and brimstone for 40 days and 40 nights it won't melt the snow enough to get your damned mail through on time.

This time the snowfall is bureaucratic in nature. Randolph was not recommending that the Senate undertake the construction job suggested by the Trotters. His concern was that there was so little public leverage on the

Postal Service. Said the Senator: "We will begin to take a more critical view of their policies, procedures and plans from now on. . . . Maybe even legislate the return of some type of legislative control so that the public can better be served."

There have been other unforeseen effects of the reorganization, beyond the contribution to inflated postal prices. The change from the public service orientation has already had a profound effect on existing and future magazines of America. The new, higher second-class postage rates for magazines place them at an increasing competitive disadvantage with respect to other media, especially in terms of advertising revenue. As monopoly in media grows in newspapers, and is fostered by government licensing policies in TV and radio, the high postal rates will reduce the significance of magazines in molding American opinion and providing an outlet for voices and views that otherwise would not be heard.

In the main the Postal Service is going in the opposite direction from the hopes of its sponsors—something like Dr. Frankenstein's experience in the monster business. (The few areas of progress, which might well have occurred regardless of the reorganization, will be discussed later.) The Postal Service is big business—big monopoly business. It would fit in as number four among *Fortune*'s five hundred with its over $11 billion per year in revenue. The reorganization, however, has cut it off from effective public control. Congress has all but stepped out of the postal picture, neither asking for nor deserving as much as a commemorative stamp. A band of quasi-business, quasi-government officials are running the Postal Service like a private fiefdom, and this will have an increasingly baneful influence on the economy as a whole. All debate on whether there may be better methods of organizing the delivery of the nation's mail has been stifled.

Modern methods of accounting (a code phrase for possible deception and subterfuge) applied to the Postal Service's annual report may help to disguise for a time the Postal Service's true financial performance. In January 1973 it was revealed that the Postal Service submitted a proposal to the Office of Management and Budget, forecasting a profit for fiscal 1974 of $56 million. The OMB pointed out, however, that the Postal Service owed the government for employee benefits since July 1, and on that basis, the Postal Service started out the fiscal year with a $278.8 million deficit. According to its annual report, the Postal Service loss in fiscal 1972 was approximately $175 million. This did not include the subsidies for various classes of nonprofit and second-class mail that have, since the inception of the postal system, been carried as a public service loss and have made up part of the controversial postal "deficit." "In total," former Postmaster General Elmer T. "Ted" Klassen said, "we received about $1.4 billion of taxpayer money." In fiscal 1973 (the year ending June 30, 1973), Klassen claimed a loss of only $13 million, with $1,410 billion in government subsidy listed as income. Fiscal 1974 showed a loss of over $400 million, plus $1.4 billion subsidy, or nearly $2 billion, a new record. The fiscal 1975 deficit is estimated at $2.3 billion. Hardly an encouraging outlook. But this is where we stand. A brief examination of the path that led to the 1970 legislation will help explain how we got here.

Postal or messenger services have been an instrument and function of government from earliest times. The government of any country traditionally established a monopoly over this vital means of communication to insure its survival against rivals. The post office, in a very real sense, was the visible symbol of imperial power. This was equally true in the early days of American democracy, as the federal government sought to impose its writ across the states and into the frontier of the Far West. By controlling the post, the government could censor activity inimical to its own interests, raise additional revenue, and offer a service to the citizens in return for their tax obligations.

In English history the postal monopoly assured that communications beyond the British Isles were handled only through messengers authorized by masters of the posts. In Cromwell's day the Post Office Act of 1657 emphasized the importance of a centralized post office as a means not only of promoting trade but of discovering and preventing "many dangerous and wicked designs which have been and are daily contrived against the peace and welfare of this Commonwealth, the intelligence whereof cannot well be communicated but by letter of escript." The latent power of the Post Office as an overt censor was exercised during World Wars I and II. This authority is generally restricted in peacetime to internal security and criminal cases authorized by the courts, but it still has the same potential against civil liberties, through "mail covers," that recent abuses of the power of wiretapping have demonstrated.

In 1753 Benjamin Franklin became the first Postmaster General for the North British Colonies in America but was dismissed in 1774 because of his sympathy with the American independence movement. After the outbreak of the Revolution, Franklin served again under appointment by the Continental Congress during 1775 and 1776.

In Colonial times the policy was to make a profit from the postal service. But after the Post Office was made a separate department of government, this policy was changed. It was felt that the department should render good service to the public with due regard for cost, but it was maintained that such service need not always be self-sustaining. Deficits, therefore, became common in the conduct of the department. By the mid-twentieth century, revenues of the U.S. Post Office Department amounted to more than $1.5 billion annually. Expenditures exceeded $2.1 billion, leaving a deficit of about $600 million.

The tradition of the Post Office as a public service notwithstanding, its yearly deficits drew fire from the more conservative elements in the Congress—those who would run the government on the same tidy basis as a thrifty housewife successfully balances the family budget. At the same time, the political patronage value of selecting 35,000 postmasters lessened as population and congressional districts increased in numbers of voters. Post office patronage, in terms of votes and campaign contributions, paled before the onslaught of corporate cash and the local party and volunteer organizations. Another serious consideration was the fact that for every happy post office appointee there were ten disgruntled aspirants.

Beyond that, for legislators with more pressing issues on their list of priorities, the post office was becoming increasingly complex to administer. The volume of mail was growing in flood-tide proportions. It was Larry O'Brien, the last of the strictly political operatives posing as Postmaster General, who sounded the alarm in 1967, insisting that cracks were developing in the postal edifice that foretold imminent collapse.

In the wondrous ways of Washington, O'Brien's complaint was referred to a presidential commission. The commission, chaired by retired American Telephone & Telegraph chairman Frederick R. Kappel, was composed of men with broad experience in everything except postal matters or the public interest. The perceptions of this group ultimately made their way into the Postal Reorganization Act of 1970, which transformed the Post Office from a public service into a so-called public utility.

To implement this change, the commission recommended replacing the traditional department with a new government corporation aimed at businesslike efficiency. One could offer with equanimity an all-expense-paid trip to Disneyland for the whole family to anyone who can name the Board of Governors of the United States Postal Service. A free Big Mac might be the prize for the first one hundred high school students who know the last name of the present Postmaster General.

The main effect of this anonymity of the management of the Postal Service is that there is no one to complain to about poor service or escalating costs. There is no way, for example, to question the wisdom of the 1973 settlement with the four major postal unions which cost well over $2 billion (except for the Pentagon, the Postal Service is the largest employer in the United States—just over 700,000 workers). One could, it is true, complain to the $40,000 per year assistant postmaster general for customer services. "I guess you would say in some ways if you have a complaint, the buck stops with me," said William B. Dunlap, who presently occupies the position. But if he doesn't act on your complaint, Mr. Dunlap concedes that there is not much you can do about it.

For the postal employees, the change of the Post Office to a "public utility," a government corporation that can sell its own bonds and earn a fixed and "fair" rate of return, was at first unsettling. They consoled themselves with the 1973 labor settlement in which the workers got 7 percent pay increases for both 1973 and 1974, plus unlimited cost-of-living increases and additional fringe benefits, despite general agreement that postal wages are higher than comparable jobs in the private sector.

At the time the labor negotiations were taking place, scenes out of the bleakest novels of Charles Dickens were conjured up by spokesmen for the workers. Nineteenth-century sweatshops apart, the idea that the Post Office was antiquated was certainly true. The effort to replace men with machines is still going full throttle—with a curious result. Over 35,000 workers (mostly part-time) were eliminated from their jobs by the end of 1972, but the complaints of poor service, delays in mechanization, and a no-layoff labor contract resulted in an actual increase of 304 full-time employees by mid 1974. The Postal Service is still labor-heavy, with only $1,145 in capital investment per employee in 1968, compared to about $35,000 per worker in telephone and telegraph. By 1972 total assets per postal worker were still less than $5,000 per employee, compared to median assets per worker of more than $25,000 among the top industrial corporations.

As it happens, replacing men with machines does not necessarily spell efficiency. According to a March 1974 report of the Comptroller General, letter-sorting machine error at Chicago was 3.4 percent. Tests showed an error factor of 12 percent. Something a little more reliable than that is required of management, and that something does not seem to have been forthcoming. For example, at the Merrifield, Virginia, mail-processing facility employees charged in a series of letters to Representative Morris K. Udall (D., Ariz.) that the Postal Service was turning the sprawling plant into a "sweat box," forcing workers to keep on the job ten to eleven hours at a time and harassing them if they refused. The list of specific complaints included the following accusations about the understaffed plant:

- Mail circulars and some other types of mail were being delivered late or not at all.
- Special delivery letters were delivered with regular mail.
- "Scare tactics" were used that resulted in three employees suffering heart attacks.
- Clerks and sorters were repeatedly given orders to work eleven to twelve hours a day, and then the orders were rescinded.

Why such bizarre personnel policies? James Rademacher, president of the National Association of Letter Carriers, realistically says that the Postal Service believes overtime payments are cheaper than salaries and fringe benefits. "All they want to do," he said, "is forestall a postal rate increase and they're driving the service deeper and deeper into the ground." In any case, overtime has shot up. In the main New York post office, for example, from January 1972 to January 1973, mail volume was up 11.7 percent, employees down 14.5 percent, and overtime up 467.5 percent.

The Merrifield plant is only one of a series of over five hundred processing plants that were the handiwork of Winton M. "Red" Blount, the first Postmaster General under the 1970 act. These new facilities are replacing many small post offices and are designed to lick the problem of anticipated mounting mail volume by higher productivity per worker and therefore lower postal costs. Or so the theory goes. Blount himself left the Postal Service after only one year to return to his native Alabama and his family construction business. To date, the effect of his new facilities has been something less than sensational, either in efficiency or in cost reductions. Representative Robert N. C. Nix (D., Pa.) has pointed out that under a new package mail-routing system, packages sent from the town of Modena, Utah, to Panaca, Nevada, 20 miles away, will travel 2,309 miles.

Just growing pains? Consider the case of another mail-sorting center now in operation in Bangor, Maine, centralizing workers and services and closing bypassed facilities. Not only have new costs been incurred, but many of the old ones remain. In Ellsworth, Maine, for example, the Bangor move left the Postal Service with a twenty-year lease at $28,000 per year on a new building no longer

11

needed. But, reports J. R. Wiggins, publisher of the Ellsworth (Maine) *American,* "it claims to have saved the salaries of four employees who have retired and who have not been replaced. Presently, Bangor is using manual sorters and paying them overtime to handle the mail that was dispatched from smaller sorting stations."

A practical sort of man, publisher Wiggins decided to test the speed of the new sorting system, which involves variations of the wrong route syndrome reported by Representative Nix. The once-a-day truck that goes from Ellsworth to Bangor for sorting, and then back to nearby areas, could take up to thirty-seven hours. So Wiggins had a friend drive an ox cart to Surry, seven miles away, with this result:

> Sancho and Pancho [the two oxen] carrying mail from the Ellsworth *American* in Ellsworth to the Jones General Store in Surry . . . made an historic run of three hours, seven minutes and 32 seconds, besting the Postal Service by 19 hours, 52 minutes, and 28 seconds, for a comparable delivery of a letter posted at the same time of day. . . . Now, it can be argued that this is of no particular concern beyond the borders of Hancock County, Maine. But a case can also be made, on the contrary, that it is an event of some considerable national significance because, in the interests of economy and efficiency, precisely the same consolidation of mail sorting centers that has taken place in Bangor is happening all over the country.

The Postal Service claims that this new system will speed up the travel both of mail originating in rural points and intended for remote urban points and of mail going from urban points to rural areas. But by the same token it has delayed mail going from one rural point to another, requiring the county mail to travel to the more distant sorting center and return. Some of the pitfalls of the new system may be corrected, but, nonetheless, automation and delivery patterns will heighten the isolation of rural life and increase the concentration of people and facilities in the 5 percent of America that is bursting with 90 percent of the population. This is the kind of mindless trend, in the name of "hard-nosed" management, that can dangerously lower the American pulse beat if it doesn't kill us off altogether.

All this reorganization is being done by the new breed of officials in the Postal Service who supposedly know where they are going. But do they? In a speech to the Magazine Publishers Association (MPA) in September 1972, the customer's friend, Mr. Dunlap, concluded his speech on this note:

> Each of us has a tendency to look at our own position as being the most important. If I have one request of you it is to look at our problems and help us solve them. I plead for understanding. I ask for time, and I ask for your unlimited cooperation to make this reorganization work. I shudder to think what will happen if it fails.

In 1973 the Postal Service moved about 89 billion

13

pieces of mail, up from 87 billion in 1972. (Volume rose to 90 billion in 1974.) The Postal Service seemed to view the growth as more of a problem than a business opportunity. Already the parcel business has been syphoned off by the privately run United Parcel Service (UPS), and private companies are clamoring for a share of the first-class letter and advertising trade. Without better performance, the Postal Service will be faced with a wide range of strong competition in moving messages. If you had lived in eighteenth-century London, you would have experienced the luxury of eight deliveries a day. In twentieth-century America, even once-a-day service is becoming problematical.

The legendary invulnerability of the postman to the natural elements derives from an ancient description of the speed, prowess, and dependability of the Persian imperial couriers in the days of Xerxes. But what nature was unable to accomplish, the new Postal Service is on the way toward achieving. In its handling of the basic communications system of America, it has placed the Postal Service interest first and the public interest second.

Both we consumers and the Postal Service itself are in for some tough times. It is clear that the present hybrid system will not work. No one can say for sure what the future will bring, but evidence strongly points to a shift back toward the old system of high public subsidies as a matter of policy, or a trend toward allowing private competition for all classes of mail. There may well be a combination of both. One thing is certain. The present system cannot last.

II

THE SEEDS OF REORGANIZATION

The history of the Post Office has been marked by a continuous tug-of-war between the urban areas, paying their own way on postal costs, and the frontier rural areas, which have been a drag on costs and kept postal rates high (and if not high enough, created a deficit). Today, as former Postmaster General Klassen put it, city dwellers "sure are" subsidizing the mail for people living in the country.

The growth in the miles of routes served, the concept of rural free delivery, the vast increases in the volume of mail following the Civil War, and the expansion of services again during and after World War I all contributed to making the postal operation big business. The Congress, each time the issue was raised, came down in favor of a deficit operation as a public service. The Post Office was a highly political animal in terms of appointments of personnel, and there was the usual chicanery in such matters as the purchase of

15

supplies and determining which local bank should have the Post Office account. But by and large the system moved the mails.

The reign of James Farley as Postmaster General in the 1930s, during the first two Roosevelt administrations, was turbulent in both labor problems and cost cutting. But the deficits were cut, and through the forties, under a variety of Democratic Postmasters General (the old campaign manager spoils system), the Post Office continued to function without much controversy.

The years of Arthur Sommerfield, under Eisenhower, were noteworthy for better relations with the long-established postal unions and for experimentation with sorting equipment, in a feeble effort toward modernization of the hand sorting, hand moving, hand delivery of the mails. But since the Post Office throughout this period usually came in last on congressional appropriations, the whole system gradually grew antiquated.

Under President John F. Kennedy, the main contribution of Postmaster General J. Edward Day was to bring a more urbane and humorous approach to the management of the mails. His unmemorable successor was John A. Gronouski, who in turn passed the torch to Larry O'Brien, LBJ's campaign manager. O'Brien thoroughly enjoyed the perquisites of being Postmaster General—the palatial office at Twelfth and Pennsylvania, Cadillac with chauffeur, and plenty of staff. As Johnson's man of Capitol Hill, however, he had little time to pay attention to the Post Office job. Consequently, when trouble struck, O'Brien was caught by surprise.

The 1950s and 1960s saw a remarkable increase in the

volume of mail. In 1953 the volume was over 50 billion pieces, hitting 60 billion in 1958, 63 billion by 1960, and 75 billion by 1966. Had this amount of increase been foreseen, some of the modernization programs might have begun in earnest, forestalling the day of crisis. But there was still no congressional incentive or administrative pressure to take that route. The net deficit in 1960 had been $637 million—not exceptional—but the volume was growing against a deteriorating system in which Congress simply would not invest money. When disaster finally struck, it was no less shocking for having been foreseeable.

The focus of the postal horror story was in Chicago, although in the autumn of 1966 the mail had begun to slow in most of the major urban areas of the country as well. In October of that year, activity in the huge Chicago post office—thirteen stories high and covering sixty acres, billed as the world's largest postal facility—stopped. For almost three weeks the mail hardly moved. Over 1 million pounds of mail, exceeding 10 million pieces, was backlogged. The situation was so bad that one assistant postmaster general seriously recommended burning the stacked-up third-class mail (commonly but incorrectly known as "junk mail") and reimbursing the senders.

Some of the following management problems were identified as causes for the Chicago debacle:

- The postmaster's job had been vacant for six months and no replacement had been named.
- Improved pensions had led to an unusually high number of retirements.
- There was low employee morale and no discipline.

17

- Sick leave was double the national average.
- Chicago had the lowest productivity in the entire nation per man-hour worked—no mean accomplishment considering the state of postal efficiency around the country.

Added to bad management were physical plant problems, again the outgrowth of the Congress' last teat philosophy on funds for the Post Office. Dock space around the Chicago facility was inadequate, forcing mail trucks to circle on down the street; the location was poor in terms of the growing dependence on truck transportation; the building, large as it was, was designed for much less volume and was poorly laid out for the machinery that had been installed there; the machinery in question was poor; there were repeated breakdowns in the conveyor belts and elevators used to move the mail about the facility; and half of the tractor fleet was inoperative because of breakdowns.

Short of burning the backlog, the crisis could only be solved by unprecedented and prompt measures. O'Brien went to the Post Office's old tormentors, the Bureau of the Budget, and got permission to borrow $30 million from the appropriations for a future quarter. He changed the overtime rules so that more hours could be worked, when and where they were needed. He made 26,000 substitute employees regular postal civil service employees, and he hired 150,000 temporary workers (something like 10 army divisions) in November to gear up for the Christmas rush.

Heroic as these measures were, O'Brien saw the handwriting on the wall. The joys of being Postmaster General were soured by the recognition that his office did finally bear responsibility to the citizens and businesses of the country—that he was personally responsible, in a real sense, for a function of government. O'Brien took this problem very seriously, although there is little evidence that anyone else did. His speech at a meeting of magazine publishers and editors in Washington, D.C., on April 3, 1967, was something of a bombshell.

What O'Brien proposed to the above gathering was a total break with the past insofar as the management of the Post Office was concerned. His proposal seemed so radical that at first no one paid it much heed, least of all Congress. The burden of the speech was simple: The Post Office is unmanageable under the present arrangements and should be abolished. Rising Phoenix-like from its warm ashes would be a government-owned, nonprofit corporation complete with a board of directors. Congress would still play a role in Post Office affairs, but a sharply restricted one. It would appropriate money for the traditional "public service" functions of the Post Office, which have been justified for almost two centuries on social and cultural (but not economic) grounds. Those include maintenance of post offices in locations that really don't merit them on a cost-accounting basis; granting special rates for newspapers and magazines to continue the spreading of information and educational light on the land; giving special rates for nonprofit organizations; allowing free mail for the blind; and so on. A new formula for postal rates would also be devised. But the main thing was that the Post Office would be managed by the new corporation.

This was a bold step indeed, and the reasons the harassed

O'Brien suggested it are summed up in this 1967 exchange in testimony before the House Postal Appropriations Subcommittee, chaired by Tom Steed (D., Okla.).

> *Mr. Steed*: General . . . would this be a fair summary; that at the present time, as the manager of the Post Office Department, you have no control over your workload, you have no control over the rate of revenue, you have no control over the pay rates of the employees you employ, you have very little control over the conditions of the service of these employees, you have virtually no control, by the nature of it, of your physical facilities, and you have only a limited control, at best, over the transportation facilities that you are compelled to use—all of which adds up to a staggering amount of "no control" in terms of the duties you have to perform. . . .
>
> *Mr. O'Brien*: Mr. Chairman, I would have to generally agree with your premise . . . that is a staggering list of "no control." I don't know [whether] it has ever been put more succinctly to me. If it had been at an appropriate time, perhaps I wouldn't be sitting here.

O'Brien had not suggested doing away with the Post Office altogether, just changing the method of management. But Congress was slow to respond, not at all certain that a change of management would lead to better service or that Congress should lose its traditional control. There was a canny suspicion that power lost is not easy to regain.

And anyway, apart from the crisis in Chicago, was the Post Office functioning all that badly?—a defensible question in the light of what has happened since.

The rural politicians were wary of the idea of running the Post Office like a business, fearing the closing of uneconomic rural post offices and the raising of rates for their constituents.

And the postal unions were equally reluctant to see such a development, fearing that with Congress out of the picture, they would have no one to turn to for wage increases and for civil service fringe benefits. On the other hand, Congress had not been dealing too fairly with them of late. They were so circumscribed by their status as government employees, without the right to strike, that they did not appear to have much real clout. (John Macy, then head of the Civil Service Commision, did not know for some years that the postal employees were part—about 25 percent—of the civil service.) George Meany, president of the AFL-CIO, would in fact have to be brought around with a fat wage increase offer for the postal unions if there were to be this kind of postal reform.

The magazine and newspaper publishers, too, would have to be convinced. They were into the Treasury trough to the tune of over $300 million annually on the heavily subsidized second-class rate. Thus they were naturally anxious that any reform would not interfere with the delivery of their publications at below cost to the Post Office.

There was a nice little bait in place for them, however: greed. In the 1967 hearings before Representative Steed's committee the postal authorities, whose estimates are notoriously bad, estimated that in 1968 mail volume would reach 83 billion pieces, or 415 pieces per capita. Considering that only fifteen years before the volume had been 53 million pieces, where would it end? Without heavy capital expenditures, automation, and high worker productivity, a veritable army of postal workers would have to be recruited and paid. Or if the rate of high expenditure on capital investment were taken, who would pay? The chances were that the publishers would have to pay higher postage rates if either of these conditions were met. Postal reorganization might just be the way to beat high postage costs.

The possibility of winning over the publishers through the above reasoning seemed excellent. Their clout in turn would be useful in influencing public opinion. Modest editorials of a forward-looking nature would help to generate the political support required to get Congress in line behind this businesslike proposal. To most publishers, businesslike is a good word, and they were willing to give it lip service.

Fundamental postal reorganization was thus an interesting idea—perhaps, in the words of the Prophet, an idea whose time had come. The question was how to develop the concept. A presidential commission? The very thing. Presidential commissions had been reporting from the beginning of the Republic on a variety of problems the President wanted to avoid. The presidential commission was a way of life.

Who should head such a commission? By chance in Washington at that moment, wrapping up a monumental study on high-level federal pay comparability, was Frederick

R. Kappel. Kappel had worked with the government in advisory capacities in communications during World War II, the Eisenhower administration, and more recently on the Ash Commission to consider how to modernize the budget and management of the whole government. A capable, mild-mannered, erect, gray-haired gentleman, Kappel had spent his whole working career in the Bell Telephone System and had literally worked his way up the pole, from lineman to chairman of the board of AT&T.

It is not to detract from Kappel's great ability to point out that AT&T is not an ordinary company. It resembles a real, garden-variety business like a wooden apple resembles a real apple. Kappel was a man who obviously would look at problems with the mental processes of one used to monopoly utility, preordaining the outcome of his study. Without any fuss he was selected, much as Mallory selected his mountain, "because he was there."

Executive Order 11341, dated April 8, 1967, appointed the commission, and Kappel set to work. As executive director, he selected Murray Comarow, former executive director of the Federal Power Commision. Comarow's sole qualification for the job by his own admission was that he didn't know anything about the Post Office. It was going to be that kind of commission. The rest of the members were there for window dressing or political reasons (e.g., George Meany, who brought with him labor's skepticism of any change that would move the Post Office away from Congress or the Postmaster General out of the President's Cabinet). The other members were George P. Baker, Harvard, Graduate School of Business Administration; David E. Bell, Vice-President, the Ford Foundation; Fred

J. Borch, President, General Electric Company; David Ginsburg, partner, Ginsburg and Feldman; Ralph Lazarus, Chairman, Board of Directors, Federated Department Stores; J. Irwin Miller, Chairman, Board of Directors, Cummins Engine Company, Inc.; W. Beverly Murphy, President, Campbell Soup Company; and Rudolph A. Peterson, President, Bank of America.

The common tie of the members was their mutual lack of knowledge about the postal business. Thus unencumbered, the Kappel Commission launched its momentous study of the U.S. Post Office Department.

III

THE HIGH COST OF GOVERNMENT SERVANTS

Historically, good postal service (multi-deliveries per day) has depended on cheap labor. The fact that Mr. Kappel served on both the federal pay comparability commission and the postal reform commission had unintended effects on the payroll cost structure of both the U.S. Government in general and the Postal Service in particular.

During his twenty years of consulting with the government, Kappel had often been struck by the need for government to pay higher salaries in order to obtain and keep key people. He had previously approached the assignment to the Commission on Executive, Legislative, and Judicial Salaries in that spirit. But he had had no way of controlling what use would be made of his recommendations or just how the final legislation would be worded. Since all branches of the government were as one with respect to benefits, it followed as night the day that the results would

25

be costly. Sure enough, the eventual legislation tied raises in top-level salaries to Civil Service salaries (the most recent being the Federal Pay Comparability Act of 1971), which in turn was tied to military pay scales. This arrangement created a vast federal pay cost overrun. On the Civil Service side alone, since 1969, salaries have risen 50.5 percent. *Each 1 percent* in pay increase costs $500 million.

Today, the Postal Service, with over 80 percent of its employees union members, cut off from the regular civil service pay schedules, is leading the way on costly pay and fringe benefits, thanks to its July 20, 1973, settlement. Mike Causey in his "Federal Diary" column in the Washington *Post* of March 1, 1974, had this to say about the salary of postal workers: "Thanks to their current contract with the U.S. Postal Service, rank-and-file employees are guaranteed regular living cost raises on an automatic basis. That contract, negotiated by the five exclusive unions, looks better all the time and is the envy of the Federal Service."

The bid by Congress in 1974 to raise its own pay by $12,500 (more in itself, incidentally, than the median family income in America) when it is finally successful will be reflected in the chain-reaction effect elsewhere in government: soaring federal and military pay costs that are as inflationary as they are wasteful. The idea of federal pay comparability contrasts sharply with the grudging efforts of the executive and legislative branches to raise the minimum wage to $2.30 per hour, which after taxes is below the family poverty level.

A good description of how the whole system works was contained in President Richard M. Nixon's message to the

26

Congress on January 9, 1973: "The American system of career civil service is based on the principle of rewarding merit. . . . One way of achieving this is to maintain a salary scale for civil servants that is just and comparable to that received by equivalent individuals in the private sector." Accordingly, he adjusted government salaries up 5.14 percent. By formula, the law called for comparable raising of military pay. The President continued:

> Concurrent with the issuance of this Executive order adjusting pay for civil servants, I have also signed an Executive order providing a pay increase of 6.99 percent in the basic pay of members of our uniformed services. This executive order complies with section 8 of Public Law 90-207 (31 Stat. 654), which provides that whenever the rates of the General Schedule of compensation for Federal classified employees are adjusted upward, there shall immediately be placed into effect a comparable upward adjustment in the basic pay of members of the uniformed services.

For the military this has had an amazing result. From 1968 to 1973, while manpower was being cut over one-third, Pentagon manpower expenditures climbed from 42 to 56 percent of the defense budget. The 5.5 percent increase for the Civil Service approved by President Gerald Ford in October 1974 translates into over 7 percent for the military.

How do these things happen? Here are Kappel's rationales

as expressed in his 1968 federal pay report, the same philosophy extending to his view of Postal Service salaries:

> The ability of our nation to meet the challenges of these troubled times depends on the leadership of those who place their talents and energies at the service of their country. It is with the maintenance of the quality of that leadership that we are concerned here. What are the incentives for able men and women to assume positions of leadership: among them are prestige, the challenge of public service, the opportunity to help solve problems of national and international import, the sense of mission to act for the public good. All are powerfully attractive. At the same time, however, salary inducements must meet the realities of personal and family obligations. They should also reflect in some appreciable degree the level of responsibility involved in the office held.

Thus the Kappel comparability proposals raised the pay of the President from $100,000 to $200,000, Cabinet members from $30,000 to $60,000, and so on. For members of Congress, the commission thought a little kicker like $20,000 from $30,000 to $50,000 would be about right. Even Congress blushed at this and settled for a 42 percent rise to $42,500. As noted in the commission's report, all of these proposed increases at the top levels would cost about $34.7 million. But no one talked about the expensive linkage that would eventually run into billions of dollars.

The pay scales also ignore the fact that even though government pay had been traditionally fairly low, this is largely offset by job security (in December 1974, federal and postal unemployment rate was 1.3 percent compared to the national rate of 6.5 percent), fairly undemanding work (except at the top), and generous retirement benefits. All these extras still exist. In an article in *The New York Times* on December 17, 1972, Edwin L. Dale, Jr., observes that on the basis of the $250 billion budget that was the administration's goal for the previous fiscal year, over $31 billion, or one eighth of the money, is committed to the federal payroll. In the past twenty years, total federal employment (including the Post Office) has gone from 2.6 million people to 2.8 million, but the growth in salaries has risen 300 percent, with fifteen pay raises in the past decade, all of them substantial (around 6 percent). Six percent of a higher and higher base leads to big money. A 6 percent increase per year, in fact, doubles a salary in twelve years. Jack Anderson has gone so far as to describe the new salary levels in the government as having created a new elite. In his column of December 20, 1974, on the economy, he put his evaluation more strongly:

> Federal employees are becoming the most powerful self-interest lobby in the country, and their demands are being squeezed chiefly out of the middle class.

The corresponding military pay hikes are vastly more expensive than they appear, since they do not take into account quarters, food, off-base housing allowances, and twenty-year retirement programs (all financed by the tax-payer). In discussing the costs of the new navy Tomcat fighter, "son of TFX," the Washington *Post* said:

> The F-14's money predicament is part of what some specialists consider the biggest problem in the whole area of national defense today—the United States is pricing itself right out of military effectiveness. This is true not only of expensive planes like the F-14, but of the American armed forces as well. Military salaries are rising to the point that a large standing army is becoming economically prohibitive.

George Wilson, of the Washington *Post,* created a mild sensation in December 1972 with a headline on the front page (not written by him): "Each Career Soldier Costs Taxpayers $1.7 Million." This raised a furor across the river at the Pentagon, whose rebuttal consisted of two arguments: They weren't costing that yet (but certainly will if things go on as they are), and besides, why pick on the military when compensation was going up everywhere else as well? Actually, although Wilson may have been a few dollars off (his figures, after all, had come from the Pentagon), the fact remains that not everyone is going to be compensated as well as the military—not everyone will get that kind of pay and retirement, not to mention the lush low-cost housing, chauffeured cars, even enlisted servants, that are among the perquisites of military rank. Here is Wilson's account of why one GI is so costly:

An 18-year-old sworn in as a private tomorrow would make over $37,000 a year if he rose to the rank of master sergeant by the end of his 20-year tour. Assuming he lived to his predicted life span of 75, he would collect almost $1.4 million in retirement pay after taking off his uniform. The rest of the $1.7 million would be paid off as he rose through the ranks.

Military retirement is paid for entirely by the Pentagon, and has cost-of-living escalators now running at 6 percent a year. In 1973 it was estimated that military retirement cost $4,325 billion of a defense budget of just under $76 billion, or 5.7 percent of the total defense budget. Retirement pay is up $2 billion from the 1969 figures when it was 3.1 percent of a $78-billion defense budget. Under current military pay scales, using Pentagon statistics, Wilson calculated that for the twenty active years of the soldier's career it would cost the taxpayer about $85,000 per year per soldier.

If at first glance none of this seems to have much to do with the Postal Service, remember that Mr. Kappel was instrumental in initiating the new pay structure, and take note of the role of the Postal Service in continuing this lunatic escalation.

Nowhere is the myth of underpayment of government servants more celebrated than in the halls of Congress. At the same time Congress has a way of not counting all its monetary blessings. Over and above the $42,500 salary, the average personal fringe benefits of a member of the House are put at $8,500. This includes pension, $3,400;

life insurance, $512; health insurance, $264; free medical care, $224; tax breaks (which are increasing), $1,918; travel, $1,000; parking, $540; gymnasium, $153; and miscellaneous, $500. Further, effective January 1, 1975, each house member's "stationery allowance" was raised by $2,250. Total "expense allowances" are now $25,480, up 56 percent. Most members of Congress receive additional monies from speaking and writing fees. Furthermore, Congress is one of the few areas in government where public servants can keep their profession or business intact while ostensibly serving their constituents full-time. According to a May 1973 survey by the National Committee for an Effective Congress, 117 of 363 nonfreshmen members of the House maintained some kind of outside income-producing professional or business connection in 1972.

A few members of Congress have tried to resist the almost uncontrolled escalation of congressional salaries. Representative Ancher Nelsen (R., Minn.) introduced legislation in the House on January 31, 1973, to abolish the Commission on Executive, Legislative, and Judicial Salaries. Unless the commission is eliminated, Nelsen said, "it will recommend salary increases for Congressmen, Senators, and other top Government officials. . . . If we desire to check inflation, then we in good conscience should not go along with this scheme that seems certain to mean pay increases for ourselves. Congress should face up to the fact that this Commission represents an unethical, backdoor method of raising the pay of National Government officials." Unquestionably, the commission method of getting pay raises is a happy one for the average member of Congress, providing him with higher pay and allowances without forcing him to vote for them publicly and risk riling less fortunate folks back home. Nelsen concluded: "When this same method was employed in early 1969, I well recall, it was impossible for us even to get a recorded vote on the pay hike package in the House of Representatives. Hence, everybody in Congress got their salary raised without having to be accountable to the voters. It is a wrong way to do business."

There would appear to be no permanent end to these higher salary costs, which, incidentally, are in no way pegged to higher performance, but rather are geared to claims of above average cost-of-living increases. In fact, government salaries from 1969 through 1973 rose 45 percent, against a cost-of-living increase during the same period of 21 percent. The Civil Service Commission and the Office of Budget and Management agreed to study private industry on the question of bonus systems and other financial fringe benefits, to see whether such items should be included in federal salary increases. One can expect the answer finally to be yes, given the way the "comparability system" works. Not only would the Civil Service Commission, as well as certain Postal Service officials, like to have a "bonus system" (akin to a "buddy system" of mutual back scratching), but the commission is even considering making the bonus tax exempt.

In its January 26, 1974, issue *Business Week* poked a hole in one of the vulnerable spots of this sweetheart system. "The people who make the survey, and those who use it, have their salaries adjusted to reflect its findings. I recognize the professional pride involved in the groups concerned, but there is surely a conflict of interest in the

33

whole process if this term means anything at all." This observation was made prior to the civil service pay experts' conclusion in June 1974 that a GS-18, the top grade, now earning $36,000, should be receiving $71,076 under the civil service comparability formula.

If the objective of the salary commission federal pay system is stability in the top levels of government, it has accomplished its purpose. Stephen Hess, a former Nixon White House staffer now at the Brookings Institution, made the following observation on the stability of the Nixon political appointees, so many of whom stayed on into the second term:

> The reasons for this unusual stability are not at all clear. I am not prepared to say that these appointees stayed on the job because they are more dedicated to public service as a group than their predecessors. Perhaps two other factors deserve consideration: the business downtrend of 1970-71 may have closed off the jobs in the private sector that high-level political executives have a right to expect will be forthcoming; and federal pay raises, bringing the salaries of Under and Assistant secretaries into the $38-42,000 range, may mean that government employment is no longer seen as such a hardship.

The same logic applies to the lower salary echelons.

The Wall Street Journal has reported that in 1965 the GNP was $648.9 billion and government spending for salaries (local, state, and national) was $137 billion. By 1972 the GNP was $1,076 trillion and government spending totaled $254 billion. Thus the GNP was up 66 percent, and government spending had risen 85 percent. Viewed in longer terms, today's GNP is eleven times larger than in 1929, but government spending is thirty times as much.

Under the Nixon administration, in spite of cutbacks in many areas, an inexorable rise in government costs occurred due to the salary formula. *Time* magazine in the August 27, 1973, issue commented that government employees (the "Prospering Bureaucrats") suffered not at all from the problems of Phases I through IV. According to the U.S. Census Bureau, Arlington County, Virginia, a suburb of Washington, with 37.6 of its wage earners government employees, has the highest per capita income in the nation—$25,446. "When there are bad times in the country, they hire more people in Washington," said the acting board chairman. William E. Colby, the CIA chief, stated on July 3, 1973, during his Senate confirmation hearings, that unless personnel costs were curbed, the agency will eventually reach a point where it will have "all personnel and no programs."

Such is the situation today, fueled by comparability legislation and the still extant salary commission. Over and above the *Business Week* survey, there is substantial professional doubt about the equity of the comparability system on any level. Joseph W. Kimmel, of Edward N. Bay and Associates, a management consultant firm that analyzes salary data for clients in private industry, reported that "civil servants, depending on their jobs, make anywhere from 5 percent to 20 percent more than their counterparts in private industry." Mr. Kimmel pointed out that in the nine years preceding 1971 federal pay more than doubled. An October 1974 U.S. Chamber of Commerce survey stated that the average federal pay of $12,984 per year was 46 percent more than the average $8,900 received in the private sector. A Labor Department survey the same time placed federal fringe benefits 12 percent higher than those in the private sector.

The scope of the inflation of government costs not only in pay percentages but in the number of higher graded bureaucrats was documented in 1973 by Peter Henle, a senior specialist on labor at the Library of Congress. His findings included the fact that the number of employees in grades GS-14 and above (excluding the Postal Service) rose from 22,477 in 1958 to 72,669 in 1971. "Part of it [the increase] is a technical government handling technical problems," said Henle, "but I don't think all of it is that way."

The result of this cost push is that the budget in many high-cost areas—i.e., the whole federal bureaucracy and the defense establishment—is already committed. If Congress is to play a meaningful budgetary role, it will have to approve and plan in five-year cycles. Only the long view will show us where pay and retirement policies are really heading, and to what extent the Postal Service, as a government corporation, is setting the pace for higher levels of uncontrolled government expenditures. It should be noted that the practice of giving all employees the same percentage pay increases means that the absolute dollar gap between the top and bottom of salary levels is increasing, which accounts in part for the fact that the bottom 20 percent of workers in America are earning proportionately less each year.

This is not to say that federal government employees or Postal Service employees should not receive pay increases. A good case could be made to pay specific people—say, the Secretary of Defense—more generously. But the present system of equal, frequent, and ever-increasing rewards for all is shattering our budget and causing the overall cost of government to get out of hand. The picture of the military drawn by George Wilson was attacked as unfair because it did not point out that other workers are subject to equally large salary increases. Such criticism is unfounded if the private sector wage patterns of the past ten years are analyzed. Furthermore, the retirement costs for the military (which are completely paid for by the taxpayer) and the civil service (now 50 percent paid for) will soar as the base pay rises, and, in the case of the civil service, as union pressures increase the percentage of government or taxpayer contribution.

Obtaining the money to fund the civil service, military, and the Postal Service at the new pay and retirement levels will tax the ingenuity of the budget planners, necessitating a new look at priorities, the hiring of fewer people, the raising of taxes, or all three.

The 1973 labor settlement of the Postal Service of 7 percent a year, with cost-of-living escalators, did nothing to alleviate a budget problem that seems to need more attention than it is receiving. In fact, the postal unions, flushed with success, are now concentrating on fringe benefits, so that the Postal Service will pay for their entire insurance package, 75 percent of the health plan (up from 50 percent), and the entire retirement plan, now split throughout the government fifty-fifty with the employee. Such a concession would add additional millions to the cost of mail delivery and by seepage, billions to the cost of the federal government.

The performance of the Pay Commission, inspired by the original Kappel chairmanship, will play an important part in determining just how far the salary levels will go before a final reaction sets in. Applicants for both federal jobs and the Postal Service are presenting themselves in record numbers.

The first important sign that the existing wage system is fatally flawed was seen in the Senate's turn-down of the Pay Commission's and presidential recommendation for yet another full-scale escalation of federal pay in March 1974. Senator Frank Church (D., Idaho), not unmindful of his fall 1974 reelection campaign, spoke out as follows:

> Is there any branch of government left that re-mains responsive to the public feeling? Let there be no doubt about it: go out among the people, where the median income is less than $10,000 a year, and tell them about the hardship which forces us to increase our salaries, when we are already in the first percentile of income in the country, and you will find out how the public feels.

The Senate vote occasioned the usual hue and cry that everyone would leave the top levels of government if there were no new pay increases. Those who departed, however, did so because the increases in the retirement system were over 6 percent and they could make more doing nothing.

This, then, is the background for the salary commission's view of government pay scales, as well as its lack of concern about where the money is to come from. It was with this same cavalier approach—higher salaries and higher charges—that the Kappel Commission on the reorganization of the Post Office settled down to work.

IV

THE REPORT OF THE KAPPEL
COMMISSION

Given Kappel's reputation for high spending on personnel, it might have been wise for the administration to direct his energies elsewhere than toward the Post Office, where, as we have seen, 85 percent of the costs are labor. Kappel's experience with the comparability pay recommendations had demonstrated what balderdash the government was capable of swallowing. This gave him little incentive to do any better in terms of the Post Office.

The product of two illusory worlds, AT&T and the swan song era of LBJ's Great Society, Kappel set out to discover what was wrong with the Post Office. His AT&T experience had taught him that he would have to establish some sort of tame regulatory setup, and from his government work he had learned that if his proposals were not expensive, they would go unheeded. The unwilling instigator, through his federal pay proposals, of a process which was to throw the entire federal budget out of kilter and help the Great Inflation of 1974, he was determined to make business sense out of the Post Office.

The Kappel Commission report was issued in June 1968. It is in some respects unbiased. On the whole, however, it was strongly colored by Kappel's preconceptions and must be read with this in mind.

The report bears the grandiloquent title "Towards Postal Excellence." It uses the 1966 Chicago postal crisis both as a takeoff point and as an omen of things to come unless the Post Office mended its ways. Larry O'Brien described the situation as "a race against catastrophe," so Chicago was indeed a good place to start.

According to one high-ranking official in O'Brien's Post Office, "the Chicago incident produced a state of panic. No administration can have the onus of saying the mail won't go through. There are still guys around the Post Office who remember the pony express and Wild Bill Cody. We took the approach that seemed both honest and politically pertinent, that is, something had to be done fast about the whole setup. The Post Office simply wasn't working to anyone's satisfaction, and that included all of us guys in it, from the letter carriers to Larry. So it seemed reasonable to appoint a commission for a new hard look to see if the problem wasn't the system itself. Kappel had just finished the pay study, was available, and no one really argued about who should look into the problem."

Against this background, Kappel rounded up his big-business and big-labor team and the "research" began. With the pot already boiling, Kappel carefully dropped in items that would make a brew consistent with his preconceptions, i.e., a postal service patterned after the Bell

Telephone System, collecting maximum rates for minimal service.

In its report, the commission touched on the problem of dissatisfaction with day-to-day mail service. The Post Office was faulted for not having more data on this problem, a common complaint throughout the Kappel report, making the commission appear as an up-to-date, research- and market-oriented body. Nor was reliable data available on what actually was sent through the mail. Kappel accepted as an article of faith that more and more mail would enter the Post Office each year. The Post Office estimated that from the 1967 figure of 78 billion pieces of mail, 1977 mail volume would hit 110 billion pieces. This would mean a 41 percent increase in volume, which, said Kappel, "gives no cause for optimism," in terms of expecting the Post Office to function effectively at such a projected volume level. One could visualize the bursting of mailbags and the roadfuls of snarled trucks hard by the sagging loading docks.

In the course of compiling its study, the commission found considerable public concern over the poor quality of mail service—delayed letters, lost magazines, damaged packages, and so on. Forty-seven out of seventy-five national associations (63 percent) faulted the Post Office in some way. "Significantly, those with special experience with a particular class of mail (e.g., second-class mail users) criticized the service given their particular class while expressing satisfaction with, or not commenting on, service generally," states the report. Merchants and housewives all complained about the mails. The commission concluded: "The lesson is clear; from a distance the mail service is not

43

bad, but the more you use and depend on it, the less satisfactory it seems."

Questions involving Post Office personnel—how people came to work for the Post Office, what they did, and what happened to them in the course of service—received special attention from the commission. One of the commission members had this comment:

> Under the present Post Office system, the individual employee is not permitted to have the opportunities that are open to employees in virtually all other private or governmental institutions.
>
> He cannot earn promotions based on merit. He is immobile, almost a prisoner of his environment, and therefore cannot take advantage of his talents and energies, except within his own tiny segment of the Department. Without political help, he cannot aspire even to leadership of his own post office. In many places, the postal employee must live under working conditions that he, his union, his supervisor, or his top management cannot do anything about.
>
> The present Post Office system fails to allow for the typical American and in fact the natural human desire to improve his abilities and his welfare.
>
> In most American enterprises, the improvements in methods and in capital equipment are the ideas of employees. Our present Post Office system effectively blocks this great potential for

improvement in postal operations. Not even the postmasters of major post offices can bring about improvements that are obvious and that would save large sums of money.

Regardless of any of the productivity improvement possibilities within the Post Office system, desirable as they may be, probably the most serious criticism is the failure of the Post Office system to offer the individual employee the kind of opportunities for personal involvement and improvement that characterizes almost every other phase of American life.

Despite this dismal on-the-job picture, the commission pointed out that the salaries paid were competitive with private companies, at least for nonsupervisory personnel. Nevertheless, the stultifying, almost militaristic hand of the *Postal Manual* determined action and response, and in effect, turned many employees into automatons in terms of originality and decision-making. The physical conditions of employment also presented major problems, as did the limited career opportunities. According to the report, "About 85 percent of all postal employees are in the five lowest grades, and over 80 percent finish their careers at the same grade level at which they start them." As for training, the average postal employee spent less than one day a year in training, mainly on his own time. It was high time that some of these facts of life were made known.

Regarding labor-management relations, the commission was especially harsh, perhaps because of its own predispositions. The postal unions were in a different situation from private unions: their members could lobby but did not have the right to strike. Further, union power was exercised not at a bargaining table, but through the Congress. In brief, reported the commission, "Congressional petition takes the place of collective bargaining."

The commission also noted that Congress simply included postal wage increases with the regular civil service increases, without regard to productivity. (Considering Mr. Kappel's role in the establishing of runaway government salaries, this was an ironic observation indeed.) Robert R. Nathan Associates, hired by the commission to report on personnel and labor relations, summed up the situation this way:

> With wages and fringe benefits determined by the Congress, management is left with the unenviable task of bargaining only the complex human relationships and conflicts inherent in such projects as the grievance procedure; promotions, reassignments, and posting of job vacancies; seniority; parking control; adverse action and appeal procedure; and advisory arbitration and optional mediation. Without the ability to negotiate basic money issues, and with the implied threat that the unions may carry their grievances to Congress, management has had little room to maneuver and has yielded bits of its authority (more than the Executive Order required) without buying union cooperation in improved management or productivity.

If the commission looked upon labor and personnel

policies with disfavor, postal finances were relegated to an even lower circle of postal malfeasance. Deficits were a way of life, and arguments that other parts of government such as the Department of Defense also operated in the red were set aside as specious. Postal services are after all sold to users, and there was no reason why charges should not equal costs. As for the public service argument, according to another of the commission's contractors, Foster Associates, only 21 percent of the total postal deficit, some 3.8 percent of total postal costs, was in the form of subsidies to nonprofit institutions and mailers of educational materials.

The high cost of postal service, claimed the commission, was unnecessary. A 20 percent saving could easily be realized (about $1 billion at the 1968 postal expenditure level) if postal management could plan and finance postal operations and capital investment. According to the commission, "There is no telling what greater savings could be made over the long pull by businesslike management in the Post Office."

This kind of seductive claim was hard to resist. It was reinforced, on the same page, by a productivity chart for 1956-66, showing at its very top Kappel's communications business with a rise in productivity of 6 percent per year, and at its very bottom the Post Office with a 0.23 percent annual increase.

Despite the lag in productivity, postal salaries had already moved slightly ahead of the economy, creating an even larger deficit. With a high capital input, however, productivity was sure to rise and the percentage of labor costs decrease. In the power utility industries, capital investment

47

was $151,710 per employee, and in telephone and tele-graph, $35,630. But in the Post Office, as before mentioned, this figure was a mere $1,145 per employee. No wonder the handcart and the individual pigeonhole still reigned supreme.

Costs and inefficiencies were the greatest in the big-city post offices, and it was here that the greatest opportunities to find large savings lay. Arthur D. Little, Inc., estimated that productivity in some cases could be increased 50 percent through the application of such existing technology as handling devices and containerization. At the same time, sorting machines already in place could be used more efficiently. There was also a need for more equipment which had not been bought because of the chronic shortage of funds for capital investment.

Approximately $5 billion would be required to provide a technological turnaround. Such reorganization would, however, take time and would necessitate the creation of a management geared toward obtaining reliable operational data from which to create a cost-conscious operation. There would also be a need for new accounting methods to determine just what classes of mail were paying their own way, and a better system for allocating the institutional costs of basic operational functions regardless of mail volume.

In the second chapter of the Kappel Commission report, entitled "The Roots of Failure," faulty management was taken to task, although the commission hastened to say that the failure here was one of method, not men. The organizational setup prevented good management, or so it would seem from the exchange between Representative

Steed and Postmaster General Larry O'Brien quoted earlier. In the commission's words:

> Because it is financed in part from the Federal Treasury, the Post Office is enmeshed in the Federal budgetary process, and thus cannot be managed as its business character demands.
>
> Because of statutory constraints, the nominal managers of the system cannot make the adaptations required by a fast-moving economy.
>
> Because of the system of selecting postal managers, normal line relations between them and top management are impossible.

In regard to the issue of Treasury financing, more urgent demands for federal moneys almost always meant that the Post Office's legitimate financial needs went unmet. In the 1969 appropriations bill, for example, although the need for postal funding was recognized by the House committee, there was nonetheless a 43 percent cut in public buildings and an 11 percent cut in plant and equipment. These financial constraints made leasing the order of the day: of sixty-seven major postal facilities built since 1955, sixty were leased. Further, with the assured deficit payment from the Treasury to fall back on, there was no customer orientation nor any effort to gather market data to see what service needs might be filled. As the commission put it: "There is little need to be concerned with customer desires if all costs are paid regardless of customer satisfaction."

Another deficiency noted by the commission was that

the rate-making function was still in the hands of Congress rather than delegated to a regulatory agency, as was the case with such "public services" as Bell Telephone and the electric and gas companies. According to the commission: "The present rate structure is mute evidence that this function should be delegated." Many decisions on what to charge for various items required technical knowledge and lay beyond the scope of the legislative process, according to the commission, which seemed to feel that Congress should be allowed to devote itself to higher pursuits, leaving the earthlings to grub as best they could in the hard-nosed world of business.

Political appointments in the Post Office also received the censure of the commission. The Postmaster General himself had averaged only thirty-one months in office, contrary to sound management continuity techniques. The role of Representatives in appointing local postmasters was considered unhealthy, with political influence rather than ability often determining rewards. While acknowledging that some congressional choices worked out well, the spoils system was viewed as a damper on employee morale, inefficient, and a cause of public lack of confidence in the Post Office.

The commission acknowledged that most of the deficiencies in the Post Office were rooted in history. The postal service had played a vital role in the opening of the West and in knitting together the farm communities with the urban centers. But times had changed. The Post Office was no longer the sole national unifier. Other communications and transportation networks had arisen, responsible to state and other federal agencies. Hence subsidized mails

50

were no longer needed. And above all, politics should be down-played in postmaster selection. Despite the changing role of the Post Office, the Postmaster General was still a member of the President's Cabinet, perpetuating an anachronism.

In analyzing the types of mail that pass daily through the Post Office, the commission did useful work. It found that correspondence between individuals was only 7 percent of the total volume (14 percent if greeting cards were included), 5 percent was business, 4 percent government, 11 percent magazines and newspapers, 26 percent advertising, and 40 percent transactions (checks, bills, statements of account, and purchase orders). Based on this breakdown, the commission argued against the existing federal subsidies, distinguishing between subsidies to the postal service as a whole, and to specified individuals or groups using the post service.

Under the first category the commission listed "rural" subsidies, funds allocated for small rural post offices which service both the needs of citizens and congressional reality and hence are justifiable. In the second category, apart from specific public service subsidies, the commission viewed what was included as mainly business mail. Attacking this, they opened the door to higher costs for many first- and third-class postage users, and especially to the second-class users—newspapers and, above all, magazines.

In its report's final chapter, entitled "A National Opportunity," the Kappel Commission recommended the creation of a postal corporation, owned by the federal government, to operate the postal system on a self-supporting

basis. It would have a Board of Governors with full responsibility, charged with "providing the nation with a superb
mail system, offering universal service at reasonable rates,
paying fair wages to postal employees and giving full consideration to the public welfare." The board was also to
establish "a basic internal organization for the Corporation, approve major proposals and provide policy guid-
ance." Board members were to have "wide experience and
detachment" (which meant that they would need to know
nothing about the postal service). The nine board members
would appoint the chief executive officer, the Postmaster
General, who also would be a board member, as would the
Deputy Postmaster General. The board would have the
power to run the Post Office, although it was envisaged
that the Bureau of the Budget and the Congress would
make a "broad annual review" of the budget.

The new postal team would set out to eliminate the
deficit through modern operating procedures. "If the Post
Office continues without change," warned the commission, "periodic rate increases affecting all classes are inevitable. Although rate increases in an era of rising costs cannot be entirely avoided, the need for them in a well-
managed postal service can be largely offset by operating efficiencies." (So far this estimate has proven to have
been one of the major misconceptions of the commission.)

Concerning personnel and labor matters, appointments
and promotions were to be made on a nonpolitical basis
and employees were to be transferred from the womb of
the civil service into a new postal career service in the
corporation. In dealing with future wage settlements, negotiations were to be made on the basis of "competing wage

levels, the principle of comparability, where possible, or a similar standard of equity." The commission granted the right to strike, if the corporation were private, but since it was public, "public agencies cannot discontinue public service." As the commission delicately phrased it: "The relative security of public employment sets public employees somewhat apart from workers in the private sector." Labor disagreements were to be solved by some kind of mediation and conciliation.

Postal rates, long a congressional prerogative, were to be placed in the hands of the Board of Governors, after hearings by expert rate commissioners, and would be subject to veto "by concurrent resolution of Congress," something a little hard to imagine. Attributable and institutional costs would be covered by a new accounting system, and each class of mail would pay its own (or attributable) costs.* The commission concluded its report by summarizing its main arguments and repeating the need for a new organizational structure which would, in turn, produce a new management. (This is, of course, pure though unintentional Marxism. Economic structures will create a new breed of men. If further evidence of the deficiencies of Marxian economic theory is needed, one need only take a close look at the result of the commission's recommendations as illustrated by today's Postal Service.) In any case,

---

*Postal costs are broken down in two ways: attributable (the direct cost of moving a given piece of mail) and institutional (the contribution to the general cost of running the Post Office—buildings, trucks, staff, etc.). Under the old Post Office attribution of costs was by Kentucky windage; under the Postal Service, the system is more accurate but still has its share of ambiguities.

53

Nietzschean "new men," management leadership, was essential. In the commission's words the Postal Service "needs a management free to manage with all that entails; authorities matched with responsibilities; a sound accounting and an information system so that they know where they have been and where they are going."

The commission devoted the remaining hundred or so pages of its report to in-depth studies, then added four volumes of annexes. Whatever one thinks of the quality of the input, the Kappel report represents a serious effort to analyze the postal system. A favorable case can be made for the commission's lack of previous knowledge of postal affairs to the extent that this gave it a fresh approach, free from old-line dogma. Whether flexibility alone qualifies a commission member to dictate policy is another question. There was no consideration given, for example, to the idea of opening the whole postal monopoly to private competition.

Nonetheless, armed with the Kappel report, the administration went to work to persuade Congress that there was, in fact, a better way to move the mail.

V

THE DEBATE OVER POSTAL REFORM, 1969

Congress welcomed the move to revitalize the Post Office with highly visible bipartisan support. Yet it was to take many months of bickering before a postal bill, acceptable to all sides, became law.

Fortunately for the advocates of postal reform, there was not much enthusiasm in Congress for the political appointment of postmasters. This highly overrated perquisite of congressional office carried with it the ongoing responsibility for performance as well as the liability of the disgruntled legions who had been passed over. Still, the Post Office was an important source of patronage and as such could be useful to an enlightened member of Congress. Something being better than nothing, there was a natural reluctance to rock the boat. Added to this was a real concern among the rural members of Congress that a new postal system, dedicated to the principle of private enterprise and a break-even policy, would cut off service to their constituencies. Other members of Congress were concerned about the repercussions of postal reform on the flow of information encouraged by low-cost second-class rates, as well as the fate of the franking privilege. Special-interest groups including commercial mailers, banks and insurance companies, direct-mail firms, religious and labor organizations, and newspaper and magazine publishers wanted a closer look at the new beast before leading the old one off to slaughter.

The hearings on postal reorganization opened in the House on April 22, 1969, under the chairmanship of Thaddeus J. Dulski (D., N.Y.). By now the Nixon Administration had taken office and Winton Blount was the new Postmaster General. Blount wrote Dulski, saying he wanted to cooperate in the hearings but that he would need more time before he could make recommendations, since his new "management team" had just been formed. Dulski, on his part, noted that complaints about Post Office costs and services were widespread, and went on to state that "there is, as well, unusual agreement among postal authorities and independent authorities upon the need for sweeping reforms in postal policies and operations." The Representative from New York felt, however, that the reforms recommended by Kappel could be accomplished by simply reforming the existing mechanism rather than shifting to a government corporation setup.

It was Representative H. R. Gross who took the most profound exception to the proposals of the Kappel Commission as well as to Kappel's role in the evolution of the federal pay comparability system. As Gross saw it, the Kappel postal reforms were likely to destroy the Post

Office "under the misguided notion they are saving it." In a firm dissenting voice he said:

> I suggest that conversion of the postal service into a corporation and delegating congressional authority over postal revenues will create chaos, the disastrous consequences of which will live to haunt us, just as we are reaping the whirlwind from our delegation of authority over salaries of Members of Congress, top officials in the executive branch, and Federal judges. I disagree with the concept of delegating authority to the executive branch to solve problems which Congress finds difficult or embarrassing. I am disturbed, too, by certain modern concepts of our form of government which requires giving away all power and authority of the legislative branch under the false guise of efficiency or economy. If we continue this reckless policy, the day will come when the people of the nation will decide they no longer need a Congress.

This insightful statement recalls a haunting observation about Congress made in the 1880s by journalist Frank G. Carpenter:

> The average Congressman thinks himself a great man, but he is only a public servant, after all. He is paid by the people to do the everyday work of their government, which is already well organized. We have now all the laws we actually need.

> If it were not for the necessity of formally pass-
> ing appropriations, our country might do better
> without Congress than it does with it.*

Gross's speech was prophetic of Congress' struggle during the past several years to regain power and influence. In
spite of his eloquent opposition to the Postal Reorganization Bill, however, Gross was generally outmaneuvered by
Representative Udall in the legislative procedures so important in steering legislation through the Congress.

There was one general area in which Gross seconded the
findings of the commission. He did in fact propose a bill to
eliminate all political control over appointments and promotions, raising the possibility of postmasters being transferred to post offices in other areas, something heretofore
unheard-of. At the local level, he thought a bipartisan
forum would be the proper way to consider postmaster
selections. To remove the Postmaster General from the
political field, he would be appointed for a twelve-year
term and have no other responsibility than to manage the
Post Office. Gross's bill provided as well for the appointment of a Deputy Postmaster General from the career
ranks, and established rotating terms for the then six assistant postmasters general and the general counsel. Free of
political strings, this type of top management would provide
badly needed continuity and should be tried before embark-
ing on such a radical step as the postal corporation. In Congressman Gross's own words: "Before we delegate to some
unknown and untouchable corporate board of directors

Carp's Washington (New York: McGraw-Hill, 1960).

our constitutional responsibilities for the establishment of post offices and raising postal revenues, let us first utilize our energies and our efforts in an orderly and constructive way."

During the questioning on his testimony, Gross was asked by Udall why he had not considered other postal problems beyond appointments, i.e., the annual pay bill, rate fixing (the most political problem of all), and labor relations. Gross responded that top priority should be given to the administrative setup and to removing management from the political arena. He was not persuaded that a corporation could attract better management than a department of government.

On the question of the perils of the change to a corporation, Gross was supported by the views of Jack R. Cole, President, Mail Advertising Corporation of America. According to Cole: "The idea of corporate infallibility is one of the great American myths. There is no reason whatsoever to believe that the Post Office would be more efficiently run by corporation types under the program recommended by the Kappel Commission than it could be run under the present organizational structure. . . ," assuming the changes that Gross proposed.

The testimony of James H. Rademacher, whose National Association of Letter Carriers represented about 210,000 of the 700,000 total postal employees, also supported the go-slower reform approach of H. R. Gross. Rademacher complained about the attacks in the press, which charged that his union did not want to give up its "cozy" relationship with Congress. Whether or not undue togetherness existed, it was true, as the Kappel Commission pointed out, that the postal unions relied heavily on their political clout in Congress to meet their members' demands rather than on direct negotiation with the Post Office Department. Hence, Rademacher favored reform via the Gross bill.

Neither Blount nor Kappel advanced any sound reasons, in Rademacher's view, for the need for a corporation. They simply made assertions. Rademacher saw the Post Office as a "service to all the American people. It is not a money-making scheme; it is not a public utility."

Rademacher also struck back vigorously at the critics of the postal deficit, showing that it had fallen to $4.22 per person in 1968 and was a good deal less than such boondoggles as the farm subsidy, the oil depletion allowance, and the defense budget. While he conceded that the deficit was probably too large, he did not see the need to get overly worked up about it. His principal argument, however, reflecting the closeness of the unions to the Congress, was that "the postal service is far too important to the people of the United States ever to be permitted to be removed from the control of the people through their elected representatives in Congress."

Rademacher went on to debunk the corporate myth that large salaries guaranteed wise decisions. He cited the Edsel and Corvair debacles in the auto business and the heavy-handed investigation of Ralph Nader by General Motors watchdogs. And if the proposed corporation doesn't work, what then? "We would be far worse off than we are now," Rademacher asserted, "because the remedies could not be quickly applied as they can be today. The hands of the Congress would be comparatively tied and the entire economy and social life of the Nation could suffer serious harm before the situation could be cured." Also bothering the unions was the idea of leaving the haven of civil service for terrain that might be inferior and less secure, always without the right to strike.

In the Senate committee, Senator Yarborough raised questions about the utility concept of the postal service. He observed that AT&T served 80 percent of the American people as a monopoly, but covered only 20 percent of the land area of America, which meant that Congress had to pass a Rural Telephone Act to guarantee rural service. He also mentioned the problems of the New York Telephone service, citing companies forced to run ads in the papers saying, "We are still in business; the fact that you can't get a call through doesn't mean that we are out of business."

Clearly there was opposition to the idea of a government corporation taking over the Post Office Department. But there was no opposition to reform. The question was what kind of reform would be best. Now into the fray stepped the Citizens Committee for Postal Reform, the brainchild of Robert Saltzstein, longtime general counsel for the American Business Press (ABP). In general, the ABP feeds on the controlled circulation subsidy, not on second-class. Representating approximately 140 trade publications with an average of 50,000, it is less enthusiastic about low second-class rates than mass magazines, emphasizing the importance of good, dependable mail service regardless of cost. On October 21, 1968, the ABP board of directors instructed Saltzstein to do everything possible to promote the proposals in the Kappel Commission report.

The Citizens Council was one aspect of Saltzstein's

lobbying efforts, with Larry O'Brien and former Republican Senator Thurston B. Morton providing dynamic bipartisan leadership. The ABP itself made no cash contributions, but ABP members like Chilton Company contributed over $2,000 and McGraw-Hill, Inc., $6,000. The influential Andrew Heiskell, chairman of the board of Time, Inc., also was a supporter and contributor to the Citizens Council, a move he later acknowledged to Mr. Gross was a bad mistake. According to Senator Yarborough, the goal of the committee was to raise $1 million to lobby the bill through.

Even the prestigious executive branch addressed itself to the postal problem, with President Nixon saying firmly: "Postal reform is not a partisan political issue, it is an urgent national requirement." Postmaster General Blount in turn stated that he was determined to preserve all that was good in the current setup and prepare for the great increases in volume of mail that were projected down the line—116 billion pieces by 1980. "With the kind of reform we are proposing," said Blount, "our present employees—as well as the mail user and the taxpayer—could and should find it possible to share in the tremendous cost savings that I am convinced are achievable if this increase in volume is handled under a truly productive, efficient, and professionally managed postal system." The only catch was that these savings were to come from a massive investment in machines and new buildings which, in the words of the President, would create "a work environment comparable to that found in the finest American enterprises." Greater efficiency plus the determining of rates by an independent commission was to make the postal service nearly self-sufficient within five years abetted by small subsidies specified by Congress and paid by the Treasury. The lure of efficiency and savings was growing irresistable.

Over on the Senate side of the Capitol, in Senator Gale McGee's (D., Wyo.) subcommittee, Senator Hiram Fong (R., Hawaii), the multimillionaire businessman, found the whole idea of the postal corporation intriguing. As he saw it, congressional review of the mails had not provided the postal service with the direction it needed "in a department like this where the powers are so diverse, and are rested in so many hands that it is difficult to have the chief executive have an efficient system."

Senator Fong's enthusiasm for the corporate approach occasioned the following illuminating exchange between the Senator from Hawaii, and Senator Yarborough:

> *Senator Fong:* I think any suggestion along the line of securing more efficiency, more centralization of control, securing more interest from a board of directors and giving the manager a freer hand in carrying out the business, is more desirable than the system that we now have.
>
> *Senator Yarborough:* I fear that the chairman has pushed this thing too far. The Post Office Department is more efficient than the Congress. If you follow that criteria, we will be leased out, including the Defense Department.

Among the magazine industry lobby groups, the before-mentioned ABP was wholly committed to the new corporation idea, while the Magazine Publishers Association, composed of the large general consumer magazines like *Reader's Digest, Look, Life,* and the newsweeklies supported it with reservations. Robert E. McKenna, president of Chilton Company, expressed the ABP's position on postal reorganization as follows:

> Unless the system is completely overhauled, the post office of the future will not be adequate to do the job. If this happens, the business press, which has no satisfactory alternate method of distribution except the mails, could be obliterated. Business publishers must rely on a dependable, efficient, and economic mail system, or perish. Of course rates are important to us. But more important is the very future of the Post Office. We are willing to pay even more postage to get the kind of postal service envisioned by the O'Brien proposal and the Kappel report. . . .

Saltzstein reinforced McKenna's statement with testimony on the treadmill effect of rate increases, followed by pay increases, the same large deficit, and no substantial mechanization to increase postal productivity. He concluded: "We visualize a post office geared not to the 19th century, but to the 21st. We believe that it is time for the system to change—totally."

The Magazine Publishers Association statement, on the other hand, was a masterpiece of contradiction, reflecting the mixed feelings held by various members of the association. It was delivered by MPA President Stephen B. Kelly, formerly publisher of *Holiday* and *The Saturday Evening*

64

Post during its final agonies. "We believe H.R. 11750 [proposed by Udall and a number of cosigners] and companion bills offer the prospect of a new dimension of postal service and warrants the association's full support." The full support was reminiscent of a recent politician's promise of 1,000 percent support. "We do have major areas of concern," Kelly continued. "We believe the Committee and Congress must confront them if you are to enact meaningful reform. These areas include: public service costs; rate-making; modernization, mechanization, funding, productivity; Postal Service Management."

As the hearing progressed, the pro and con arguments in the House were largely repeated in the Senate. It will suffice to focus on two representative testimonies.

Former Postmaster General J. Edward Day struck out vigorously at the Kappel report. The fact that Day was one of three former Postmasters General testifying gives evidence of the office's high turnover. Speaking as the representative of the Associated Third-Class Mail Users, Day's principal argument with the findings of the commission was that the break-even goal, rather than service, received top consideration. He was also worried about the prospect of runaway labor costs, since he felt that concern for greater job opportunities would surely lead to higher pay scales. Day's apprehension was reinforced by the testimony of former Postmaster General Gronouski, who also saw the reorganization as a move toward higher salaries for postal workers (although Gronouski thought this was desirable).

Both Thurston Morton and Larry O'Brien submitted statements before the hearing on behalf of their Citizens

Committee. O'Brien directed his argument toward answering three specific questions posed by opponents of the administration's bill: 1. Was it necessary to go so far? 2. How would the public interest be protected? 3. How would employee rights be protected? He responded as follows. 1. In terms of efficiency, the postal corporation with large investments in capital improvements and business-oriented management would be able to straighten out the present tangled mail system. 2. The proposed corporation charter, granted from Congress and with a Board of Governors selected by the President, had enough safeguards to ensure the public good. 3. The change to negotiation between labor and management rather than a constant battle over wages and rates in the halls of Congress was devoutly to be wished.

Labor was finally induced to support the reorganization by promising George Meany a 14 percent pay hike in 1970 for postal workers, exclusive bargaining rights for the AFL-CIO (which meant the nonrecognition of several smaller unions), and the promise of real collective bargaining with the new Postal Service. In Meany's view, the postal employees would have the right to strike if necessary, even if this was technically illegal. As he put it:

> As far as the question of strike, Mr. Congressman, it is really academic. Federal workers are barred from striking by the law. But whether or not they strike has nothing to do with what is written in the law. The proof of the pudding is that they will strike. Federal, county, state, and municipal workers will strike, no matter what

you put in the law, if they do not get a fair deal from the employer.

The magazine and newspapers still had worries about their second-class subsidy, which they defined as falling in the "public service" category. But according to Postmaster General Blount, "Our approach to this matter of public service is that this is something that is up to Congress. Whatever Congress determines regarding public service, we propose that the corporation provide that public service." This reassured the second-class users that the status quo could be maintained through the time-honored technique of sound lobbying.

On July 1, 1970, the McGee-Fong bill, S-3842, became law. The public interest would be protected by the fact that the chairman of the Board of Governors was directly responsible to the President. The Postal Service, under the Board of Governors and with the Postmaster General as a board member and chief operating officer, would have authority for long-term modernization of the Post Office. To this end it could borrow up to $10 billion rather than having to rely on congressional appropriations. Finally, under the terms of the bill, the independent rate-making commission would be composed of professionals who would determine rates that paid for the costs of service, "less 10 percent [of the fiscal 1971 budget, or $920 million] which is the congressional allowance for the public interest sector, the rural areas, the 25,000 post offices out of the more than 30,000 that lose money. The significant provisio of our bill [is] that Congress in no way is to be involved in rate making. . . . We believe it is best to keep this totally independent of the Congress."

Wayne Fuller, in his excellent account of the problems and growth of the United States Post Office, *The American Mail* (Chicago: University of Chicago Press, 1972), places the Reorganization Act in this perspective:

> Tired of the responsibility of managing the postal service, unwilling to find the money necessary to rebuild the old establishment after so many years of neglect, and most of all worried about the postal deficit, which even in 1970 still did not claim nearly as much of the government budget as it had in 1890, Congress gave up its control of the system, not even bothering to keep its veto power over increases in postal rates.

And so on July 1, 1970, the brave new postal corporation was born. The official changeover would take place exactly one year later, hopefully bringing with it a New Look in the mails.

VI

THE REORGANIZATION OF THE POST OFFICE—MANAGEMENT AND MONEY

It is rare that the advice of a presidential commission is heeded. The report of President Nixon's commission on pornography, for example, was denounced by him before it was even published. The Kappel Commission report, however, had a profound effect on the Congress, and despite initial opposition on many fronts—labor, rural legislators, magazines and newspapers—wound up with full support. Even more surprising, Frederick Kappel was appointed a member of the Board of Governors of the new postal corporation and later was elevated to chairman upon Blount's departure, taking over on December 1, 1971. Kappel would play a key role in seeing that the recommendations of his commission were implemented.

As we have seen, the Kappel Commission had insisted that savings of about 20 percent, approximately $1 billion, could be made through more efficient processing techniques. Obtaining and installing modern postal machinery, however, was obviously a long-term project, so the initial concentration by the new management team was to streamline the regional setup. One of the senior post-masters general explained the take-over situation as follows:

> The main management problem under the old post office was the uneven quality of workers, which had resulted in the *Postal Manual* way as the only way to do business. This was essentially an authoritarian system. Consequently, in the whole post office, there was no executive development program, no market research, and so on, none of the things that a business-oriented management would normally institute. And as the gains in mail volume show, it would no longer be possible simply to overwhelm the problems with labor.

He went on to discuss the problem of instilling easily understood goals in the service. Whereas in the case of government goals are based on political imperatives and in ordinary business on economic gain, the aims of the post office are more complex. As he put it: "When the people understand that their careers depend on giving good service and keeping complaints down because of that service, then the Post Office will turn around in a hurry." This was the new team's answer to the old complaint that the old team didn't care. But since the deficit was always made up, what incentive did anyone really have?

There were additional difficulties. According to another senior official who had served with the Post Office and was now with the Postal Service, the two main problems of the old Post Office were untrained management and fear of risking innovation. The first problem grew out of the centralized operation of the postal system. Because of the antideficit provisions of the federal budget, the Post Office had to keep a tight grip on its network, sending out orders to all hands to hold back expenditures or speed them up depending on available funds. Thus, in a tight financial squeeze, headquarters might advise all post offices to refrain from processing third-class mail over the weekend, or forbid overtime. This prevented individual postmasters from learning to take responsibility.

Regarding the second problem, since most Postmasters General expected to be in office only a year or two, they tended to take the short-term view. Thus innovations which implied risk and possible criticism were avoided. Marvin Watson, LBJ's last Postmaster General, was an exception to the rule during his brief tenure. At one point, for example, he placed three simultaneous orders for optical scanning equipment, despite the possible criticism for duplicating efforts. His aim was to increase the possibility that a workable model be found and improvements quickly begun.

It was in the top-priority area of reducing labor costs that the new management began to show its stuff. The worst fears of the postal unions were soon realized as the twin goals of the Postal Service—in the words of former Postmaster General Ted Klassen, "improve the quality and reliability of mail services . . . and reduce costs"—were pursued. The first step in cost cutting was to lop off people. In the name of "decentralization," the regional post

71

offices were reduced from fifteen to five, with seventeen districts per region.

The people at regional headquarters represented the most experienced and senior people in the post office, a source of possible contention for management power as well as a drain on the budget. Under the new system the number of regional employees, many of them medium-level staff, was reduced from 6,500 to 3,500. By June 30, 1972, some 7,155 employees had taken the early retirement route, 1,145 had departed on grounds of disabilities, and 10,000 had left under the traditional civil service retirement plan. A manpower freeze was then instituted with all promotions made from within, thereby assuring a reduction in postal costs without much consideration of what this might do to service.

The above figures are those announced by the Postal Service annual report in December 1972. According to another senior assistant postmaster general in April 1973, there were 19,000 early retirements and 14,000 vacant positions remained unfilled. This meant that in 1970 there were 741,000 employees and by November 1972, 670,000, or a reduction of 71,000 people. Thanks to the December 1972 Christmas mail crunch, which triggered a congressional investigation in the spring of 1973, by April 1973 the number of employees was up 10,000 to 680,000. The 1973 annual report of the Postal Service showed employees up to 701,051. In 1974 the number was 710,433, up 1.3 percent.

According to one senior postal official, postal efficiency is increasing because of training and mechanization. He claims that 54,000 man-years fewer are needed today to move the same amount of mail which under the old system might have required 50,000 man-years more. Based on this "new math" principle, the Postal Service is saving about $1.5 billion (figuring $14,100 per man-year at 1975 budget estimates) over what costs would have been otherwise.

The drastic job cutbacks undertaken by the new postal management naturally generated many complaints from longtime postal employees, both directly to the Congress and to the postal unions (which in turn made tracks for their favorite member of congress). Blount faced this problem squarely, sending letters on January 12, 1971, to all postmasters saying that they were not to communicate with their local members of congress, and that all congressional inquiries to the Postal Service were to come through a designated congressional liaison officer. Blount and the present Postal Service were deeply committed to getting politics out of the post office, largely by keeping the legislative branch at arm's length. This would prove difficult, however, since the money and people of the Postal Service represented a financial and organizational base that would always be involved in politics.

Blount's strategy vis-à-vis Congress quickly raised congressional hackles. The following exchange in a House hearing on March 11, 1971, illustrates the temper of the times.

> *Albert W. Johnson (R., Pa.):* We are glad to welcome you back, Mr. Blount, in your maiden appearance as the head of the new Postal Service. I would say it has made quite a change. I know when I used to go into a post office, there was supercongeniality. Now, I am just one of the persons that put mail in the slot.

> *Mr. Blount:* I didn't know we had made that much progress, Mr. Johnson.

And again:

> *John H. Rousselot (R., Calif.):* Mr. Postmaster General, I am happy to report to you that the postmasters have taken very seriously your memorandum not to talk to Congressmen. Whereas I used to be a welcomed visitor in your post offices, I no longer am. The message has gotten across.

In response to continuing criticism by congressional members that they, as elected officials, were kept from dealing directly with Postal Service officials, Mr. Blount said:

> Nothing is perfect in this world. We will make mistakes as we go along, and we will try to correct them. But our intense effort is to be not only non-partisan but nonpolitical in the operation of the Postal Service.
>
> The operation lends itself to management as an efficient nationwide utility, but it is going to take great understanding on the part of the members of Congress as we make the drastic changes that must be made.
>
> Again I say to you I recognize that these changes represent a sharp departure from the ways in which the Members of Congress have related themselves to the Postal Service in the past. But the changes will free this committee,

for instance, to deal with its oversight functions, and to examine the broad policies and directions of the Postal Service rather than getting involved in its day-to-day operation, as has been the custom in the past.

According to the Kappel report, as we have seen, another weakness in the old Post Office was lack of capital investment in terms of construction and equipment. As a general contractor, Blount moved quickly to develop the kind of facilities required for new mail-processing methods. The old Post Office was way behind in building, and in fiscal 1972 about $725 million was obligated. Construction costs in fiscal 1973 were $402 million for new post offices which could be adapted to future mechanization programs. An additional $17.5 million was spent for building purchases, and capital building improvements totaled $65.5 million. Mounting deficits, however, are delaying actual construction. The postponement of $250 million of building projects was announced in October 1974.

There are two main programs requiring major construction currently under way. The first is the new bulk-mail system, and the second is the modernization and replacement of present postal buildings. The bulk-mail system will consist of twenty-one major centers and twelve satellite facilities equipped to process packages, magazines, catalogs, books, and advertising mail. Investment in plant and machinery will amount to about $1 billion. The first of these bulk-mail centers to be operational in 1974 was in New York City. The whole system is scheduled to be in operation by the end of 1975.

The bulk-mail program caused and is causing uneasiness in different quarters for a variety of reasons. The Postal Service fears there will be little growth in mail volume in the near future. Second-class mail, for example, was down to 9,033,839,000 pieces in fiscal 1973 compared to 9,493,992,000 the previous year. The gamble here is whether the new bulk centers will be able to take substantial parcel post (fourth-class) business away from the UPS, which now handles over half of the fourth-class mail (excluding books and records). Depending on how the rate base is figured, the rates for the new facilities may remain higher than UPS, in which case no new volume is likely to develop. UPS in turn is concerned that rate adjustments might force it into an unfavorable competitive position, while second- and third-class mailers fear that in order to pay for the new facilities rates will continue to climb, thereby raising the possibility that they, too, may be forced to consider alternate delivery. From any point of view, this major investment, leaped into without proper testing, is reminiscent of a Department of Defense weapons procurement program rather than a "hard-nosed" business operation. A Government Accounting Office report to Congress on November 1, 1974, reinforced all these worries.

The same kind of risk may be run in the development of the Preferential Mail Service, the most ambitious mail project considered. This program is to automate and speed delivery of first-class letters. It could be described as the first-class counterpart of the bulk-mail system, which is to expedite second-, third- and fourth-class mail. The estimated cost of the Preferential Mail Service, based on unproven equipment, is about $4 billion. The Postal Service has obviously kicked over the traces in terms of risk policy of the old Post Office, which reads as follows:

> Mail handling operations to be mechanized are committed to proven mechanization. Proven mechanization is that which has demonstrated its effectiveness under operating conditions. This provides the only reasonable position from which to judge the potential of postal mechanization, while avoiding the hazards of full commitment without full knowledge.

In line with this new emphasis on innovation, concern was expressed in the report of the Senate Committee on Post Office and Civil Service in March 1974 over whether the Letter Sorting Machines would work, what it would cost to keep them repaired, and whether mail volume in fact would require such techniques. The current Letter Mail Code Sort System (LMCSS) requires massing of a great volume of mail to allow effective use of the capacity, but the error rate makes the whole costly experiment dubious.

The Senate report cautioned that "although mechanization has great potential for effecting cost-saving reductions in the budget of the Postal Service, it can also become the vehicle for financial disaster. Because of the immense capital investment a worthwhile venture in mechanization will require, consideration of all the potential gain and losses must be firmly and objectively evaluated within a realistic context."

Part of the crisis atmosphere of 1966 stemmed from the knowledge that post offices were mausoleums, poorly designed for the mail system of tomorrow and inadequate for the service of today. Many post offices are at least seventy years old. Even prior to reorganization, 40 million of the 140 million square feet of postal facilities were estimated to be obsolete. Funds for building always came at the tail end of the appropriations bills, and even if such funds were appropriated, the delays in letting contracts for actual construction or modernization often dragged on for years. Not only was this an area in which the Postal Service could make vital progress, it was also a relatively easy way in which to look good by playing the ever-popular numbers game on Capitol Hill. "In 1972, we committed $393 million to the [rebuilding and modernization] program." Klassen said. "This is more than three times the annualized average of $130 million that was appropriated for this purpose in the 13 years prior to Postal Reorganization. We have budgeted $809 million for construction and modernization this year." And construction is now done with future mechanization in mind, slowed now by runaway deficits.

Another hitch developed in the construction program when the Corps of Engineers was ordered to be phased out of the picture beginning in March 1973 as the result of budget cuts by the OMB. As the Postal Service says, "This represents a serious setback to the efforts of postal management to improve mail service through modernization and mechanization since it will delay some projects." Getting the corps into the postal construction program in the first place had occasioned heated debate in 1971 when

Postmaster General Blount revealed the program to Congress with the bulk-mail facility plan thrown in as a surprise package. In Blount's words: "Construction of this bulk mail network will, we believe, enable us to operate the postal system for about $310 million less than it would cost us if we continued to do business the way we are today."

Equally surprising to Congress was the planned role of the Corps of Engineers, part of a compaign Blount had been waging to assert his independence from congressional control. When Representative David H. Henderson (R., N.C.) present at the hearing expressed concern about the news, Blount explained (if that is the word):

> Mr. Henderson, we have been considering this matter for well over 15 or 16 months. We have underway several facilities as to which the Corps of Engineers have been providing these services for us for a great number of months, as much as a year possibly. I am not certain the first time we utilized their services, but we have been negotiating and discussing these matters with the Corps of Engineers for quite some time.

It developed that Blount had signed a three-year agreement with the corps on March 11, 1971, the very day of the hearing. No, there had been no consultation on this; Blount simply stated that the Bureau of Facilities of the Post Office was not big enough to do such a large job, and that the Corps of Engineers was.

> *Mr. Henderson:* Are you satisfied that the

corps has the capability to meet this challenge in the future and in the timetable that you envision?

Mr. Blount: I have no question about it, Mr. Henderson. Prior to coming here, as you know, I spent my life in the construction business. A substantial part of the business that I performed was with various government agencies, and I worked for many of them.... A major operation such as this, it seemed to me both wise and prudent to utilize a professional organization that already had in being the kind of capability that was needed by the Postal Service.

Representative Udall could not help wondering about the long haul. After the first spurt of construction, he suggested, it might be more efficient for the Postal Service to build up its own construction capability. But Udall's advice went unheeded. When the agreement with the Corps of Engineers finally lapsed, it was decided to go out and negotiate with "reputable construction firms to take charge of the program." And that is where the matter stands today. The program continues and construction arrangements will be worked out as required in each of the five postal regions. Besides cutting into the UPS business, the new bulk-mail facilities will relieve the congestion caused by the 500 million parcels handled by outmoded facilities designed for letter mail.

The Senate report of March 1974 provided the following epithet for the Corps of Engineers program: "The retention of the Corps of Engineers to effectuate the Service's new facilities program and the termination of the

Corps' support function have caused a serious delay in the Service's effort to modernize and renovate and have brought about delay in the mechanization program."

As regards new processing equipment, orders have been placed for 1,108 letter-sorting machines since October 1971. An advanced optical character reader can sort more than 1 million letters during its normal twenty-hour operating period. The bulk of this machinery will be placed in the Area Mail Processing Centers, to which mail from small post offices is sent for processing and distribution. Centers such as these are responsible for some of the incredibly long trips mail intended for nearby points must now take, as highlighted by Sancho and Pancho's competitive run. As for the advanced Letter Mail Code Sort System, it is estimated that it can be used effectively in twenty post offices at most.

Yet another modernization project is a new headquarters conceived in the best tradition of Parkinson's that a dying institution engages in the most splendid building projects. Some $30 million was spent for a new building in L'Enfant Plaza, Washington, D.C., a lush office, residential, and shopping complex. Queried about the building, Senior Assistant Postmaster General Benjamin Franklin Bailar (now Postmaster General) answered that there were 362 feet per person at the old elegant Postal Service headquarters, about twice as much as needed. Renovation costs for the huge old-fashioned offices were estimated at $16 to $18 million. According to Bailar, the cost of staying in the old building was out of line, thus the move to the new building was actually an economy measure.

All of the above building and equipment cost a great

deal of money. Yet in spite of the fact that under the government corporation arrangement the Postal Service has the authority to borrow up to $10 billion, so far it has only raised $750 million through the private offering of bonds, an activity that has raised yet another storm of criticism and controversy. In January 1972 the Postal Service placed the first $250 million issue at interest of 6.875 percent. Salamon Brothers, the underwriters, made the usual profit. Peter Flanigan, then a presidential assistant, was widely understood to have led the Postal Service to Salamon Brothers, and the Salamon Brothers, in turn, used Mudge, Rose, the old Nixon-Mitchell firm, to handle the legal work.

Apart from the whiff of special interests in the transaction, the Postal Service could in fact have gotten funds directly from the Treasury with no interest charge. This was not done, according to one senior assistant postmaster general, because it was feared that the Treasury Department would gain too much control over the service. In testimony before the House, James W. Hargrove, a former senior assistant postmaster general, explained that another reason for selling the bonds was to bring them to the attention of the investment community. To date, the bond financing program has not played much part in the progress of the Postal Service; it may be of more value if the Postal Service reaches a break-even point, appears a sounder prospect for meeting higher interest payments, and needs more money for capital improvements. Given the break-even philosophy, however, postal bonds would not appear to be a particularly good investment, especially in today's money market.

Possibly the greatest change of all brought about by the commission has occurred in the Washington headquarters management. There were five assistant postmasters general in the old Post Office. Under the reorganization, the number ballooned to twenty-three, then settled back to seventeen, plus five senior assistant postmasters general.

Under the old Post Office, the assistant postmasters general were paid approximately $20,000, a figure that has been doubled by the new corporation. Representative H. R. Gross has repeatedly taken exception to these pay scales causing embarrassment by documenting his charges with specific examples. In 1973 his survey showed that only one of the top postal officials was earning less than he had elsewhere, while 152 others had received substantial increases. Furthermore, at least ten of these high-ranking officials came either directly from American Can Company or were "laundered" through another job en route from American Can to the Postal Service.

The "new management team" is large, increasingly expensive, constantly attending internal conferences in hotels and motels, and partial to plush offices and big automobiles. It operates in an atmosphere of mutual suspicion. Many senior officials have quietly come and gone—there have been five assistant postmasters general for public information in five years, and three for congressional liaison in four and a half years. The present combination of high pay and a depressed economy keeps most high officials in place, or shuffling from one high position to another, as best witnessed by Mr. Bailar replacing Mr. Klassen on February 15, 1975.

Compared to the austere, almost antiseptic, atmosphere

in the New York headquarters of the UPS—a company doing over $1 billion of parcel post business a year—top Postal Service seems to represent a kind of "conspicuous consumption" that belies its goal of better service at lower costs.

Jack Anderson, in July 1973, reported a few items in the lavish new postal offices: The Postmaster General's office sports a $5,290 pantry, $4,602 hand-woven African drapes that can be pulled by remote control, and approximately $6,000 worth of additional furnishings while the Board of Governors conference room features doors costing $3,550, a $3,718 chandelier, and a $50,000 kitchen in which to prepare the governors' monthly luncheon.

Mail users, harassed by rapidly rising postal rates, cannot help but view such splendor with a jaundiced eye.

VII

**POSTAL REORGANIZATION—
AREAS OF PROGRESS**

It would be foolish to deny that in some areas, the Postal Service has made progress. Whether it has made enough progress to offset its deficiencies is another matter.

There are three specific areas of Postal Service activity which merit special recognition. These are the training program for postal employees run by Director Eugene C. Hagburg, the Inspection Service under the firm hand of a former CIA security officer; and the Office of Consumer Affairs, where efforts are being made to treat mail users as though they were customers.

THE POSTAL SERVICE MANAGEMENT INSTITUTE

One of the goals of former Postmaster General Klassen, continued under his successor, is to provide more meaningful careers for his army of postal employees. In the old Post Office, the average employee received about one day per year of craft-type training, most of which was on his own time. Hagburg's Postal Service Management Institute in Bethesda, Maryland, epitomizes the improvement in the training process under the new Postal Service. Over and above its function of training employees at all levels, there is a symbolic quality about the institute that inspires workers to strive toward a high level of managerial skill. Much of the conceptual thinking about the Postal Service is being done in the institute, and what is decided there will have a long-term molding effect on the future of the mails. In addition, through the PSMI staff and their consultants, many specific problems of moving the mails are analyzed and solved, leading to substantial savings as well as improved mail delivery. The cadre of postal personnel trained by the institute will be of value however the mails are ultimately handled.

Central to Hagburg's approach in creating new men for the new Postal Service is the concept of O.D., or organizational development. This includes a Management Development program, which trains personnel to use management resources (men, money, and materials) in the most effective way, thereby improving the productivity and performance of the Postal Service. From 1968 through fiscal 1972, about 3,500 senior managers went through this training program, with the number now at about 500 yearly. Other courses of study include Unified Communications, Advanced Management, and Human Resources Management, long a sore spot among the postal employees and their unions. This latter course is directed toward getting the right man on the right job, keeping him available for work, stimulating his will to work, increasing his capacity to produce, and using him fully for essential tasks.

An important aspect of Organizational Development is the building of TEAM (Team Effectiveness Approach to Management). Through this technique, Hagburg hopes to change what he calls "dependent" organizations into independent ones. The TEAM approach is generally practical in major post offices whose large-scale problems call for substantial know-how. In addition to major TEAM efforts, however, organizational specialists from PSMI are available to sit down with the manager and staff of any post office to develop independent approaches to the problems at hand.

The many success stories surrounding the Organization Development program show that with a creative, non-*Postal Manual* approach, improvements are possible. For example, in large post offices, the lobby area may extend a whole block, with various services available at individual windows. A customer must wait in line for each separate service, and because the traffic flow is unevenly divided, some clerks are overwhelmingly busy, while others give the Postal Service a bad name by standing idle. In one such office an in-house TEAM, assisted by the regional industrial engineer and the PSMI staff, suggested installing modular units in several services to better utilize the floor space and people. The resulting personnel savings came to $49,000, against a total cost of $5,000, and 1,840 square feet of space was freed for other postal uses.

Basically, O.D. is trying to do away with some of the intellectual stagnation that impedes progress in postal operations. Thanks to a Methods Improvement course, for example, one official discovered that his post office could bypass eight handlings of loose pack mail on the way to the letter-sorting machine, at a savings of about $5,600 per year. In another case, a team devised a slide for moving sacks from a dock to the basement, thus freeing the only elevator for other work and saving about $12,000 in man-hours per year in the process.

The TEAM approach has also paid off in the problem area of absenteeism. Annual leave among managers is typically twenty-six working days. Sick leave accounts for another six to eight days, while simple absenteeism runs to an additional ten. At one major post office, absenteeism accounted for about 3 percent of the daily work force. The postmaster put several management teams to work on this problem. Special pay locations were set up for all absent employees whatever the cause of their absenteeism —maternity leave, injury on duty, union representation, special projects, pending disability retirement, Postal Alcoholic Rehabilitation (PAR), and so on. These special pay arrangements allowed management to identify the real AWOLs (absent without leave) and get them back to work, be terminated, or in some cases be retired or rehabilitated. Within two years, this metropolitan post office was able to reduce the LWOP (leave without pay) hours per accounting period from 80,000 to 45,000 man-hours. Other economies came about because of reduced disciplinary problems, not having to train new employees, and more efficient work scheduling. Savings were estimated to be in excess of $250,000.

Another PSMI innovation is the Postal Employee Development Centers. As the Postal Service becomes more mechanized, an increasing number of jobs will require technical maintenance skills. Through taking courses at the centers or by correspondence, an employee may qualify to take the advanced PSMI program which offers courses in all phases of management, including financial management, customer services, delivery and collection services, procurement, employee relations, engineering, safety systems, logistic management, and mail processing.

Hagburg is exceptionally well qualified to handle the PSMI, having a doctorate in industrial sociology backing up his many years in the field. He has every right to be proud of his program's results. During the great decline in mail service in the fall of 1972, which promoted the spring and summer 1973 congressional investigations of the Postal Service, those post offices which lost the least in efficiency and were the first to recover to normal standards were those in which large-scale training efforts had been made.

THE INSPECTION SERVICE

A second bright spot on the postal scene is the aggressive Inspection Service. William J. Cotter left his GS-16 position with the CIA to move over to the Postal Service as chief inspector, lured by a fat pay raise. A big, cheery fellow, the type one associates with British police inspectors about to bring in Jack the Ripper, he has compiled an excellent investigative record—both internally, in terms of keeping down mail theft, and externally, in catching the hardy breed that continually try to use the mails to defraud the public. He also oversees the internal audit operation and the controversial "mail cover" of suspects.

Another important area of security progress has been in reducing the number of burglaries of post office buildings themselves. With the appearance of stamp fences came the possibility of profiting from stamp robberies. Burglary losses passed the $500,000 mark in 1964; by 1967 they had risen to almost $2 million and by 1970 had attained what Cotter expects will remain an all-time high, $3,203,449. In 1971 the reduction in burglary losses became a major target of Inspection Service attention. The arrest and imprisonment of major stamp fences, the break-up of several large burglary gangs, and improvements in physical security at post offices all helped to reduce losses, which fell to $1.3 million that year. Fiscal 1972 saw losses go down to $471,000, and in fiscal 1973 this figure was reduced to $343,078.

Tracking down post office burglars has not been without its dramatic moments. One Midwest robbery attempt involved the entering by torch of a safe containing $300,000 in stamps and $7,000 in cash. The burglars were apprehended but released by error from a local jail. One fugitive fled to a remote area along the Colorado River in the state of Washington. On January 31, 1972, a force of postal inspectors, sheriffs' deputies, and state officers recaptured him in an operation utilizing a light plane for surveillance and a boat for passage through ice-clogged waters.

In 1967 the high incidence of mail theft at airports showed that organized crime was now involved. Thanks to the Inspection Service the number of parcels lost fell from

566,000 in fiscal 1971 to 451,000 in fiscal 1972; letters lost in fiscal 1971 were 246,000 and 233,000 in 1972. Cotter's investigators are working hard to reduce these totals, and are using trained polygraph teams to ferret out culprits. Postal employees arrested for theft, rifling, or other criminal handling of mail totaled 1,396 in fiscal 1972, representing a drop of over 17 percent from the previous year.

Arrests and convictions for mail fraud have shown a steep rise under Cotter's administration. That this is a tremendous area of crime is attested to by the fact that 125,000 complaints of alleged mail fraud were registered in 1972, of which 12,500 cases were investigated in the field by postal inspectors. A total of 5,200 fraudulent or borderline schemes were unearthed and thwarted as a result of these investigations, and criminal prosecutions reached an all-time high, with 2,350 convictions.

One notable haul of the Inspection Service was former governor of Illinois Otto Kerner, Judge of the U.S. Court of Appeals, 7th Circuit. He and codefendant Theodore J. Isaacs, sixty-one, were each sentenced on April 19, 1973, to three years' imprisonment and fined $50,000 on charges of violations of the Internal Revenue Code, conspiracy, perjury, and mail fraud. The indictment charged them with secretly buying shares (while Kerner was still governor) in Illinois horse racing corporations at well below the true market value and conspiring to sell the stock for large profits. A joint investigation conducted by the IRS and the Postal Inspection Service resulted in the first indictment and conviction of a sitting federal judge in the nation's history.

Auditing post office financial operations is another responsibility of the Inspection Service, and many substantial savings have been made through its audit recommendations. In fiscal 1972, alone, audit reports showed revenue deficiencies in 2,151 post offices and other shortages involving over $300,000 in official funds. Auditing payrolls, reviewing the books of procurement and contracting officials, and conducting service investigations on various consumer complaints are other duties of Cotter's organization often resulting in improved service.

Catching criminals wins loud applause, of course, but the use of the powers of the postal inspectors as an investigative tool could be a matter of concern, because of its potential to encroach on individual rights. Chief Postal Inspector Cotter defends the use of his Mail Cover System as "one of the greatest, cheapest, simplest techniques to find out leads." True enough, but ever since the abortive internal intelligence scheme revealed by the Watergate hearings, members of Congress and others concerned with individual rights are breathing a little heavy. Charges have been raised that the mail of both Senators Edmund Muskie and Hubert Humphrey was opened, read, and in some cases delayed.

According to Cotter, about two hundred "mail covers" —the listing of all mail the individual receives, noting return address and the contents—are in operation at one time. The possibility for good and evil on a grand scale lies in the power of the Postal Service to open mail. Keeping this power under proper scrutiny is certainly a task for the President, but it is almost as certainly one for the Congress as well, assuring that someone will watch the watchman.

As the Watergate tapes show, when President Nixon wanted to know for certain about Senator George McGovern's campaign contributions, he decided to use the Postal Service. There is this conversation on a September 15, 1972, tape between the President and Bob Haldeman. "P. I don't think he is getting a hell of a lot of small money. I don't believe (expletive deleted) Have you had the P. O. checked yet? H. That is John's area. I don't know. P. Well, let's have it checked." Just who did that dirty work on the Postal Service end has not been revealed.

THE CONSUMER ADVOCATE

The third organization of promise is the Consumer Advocate. It is yet to be established, however, whether such an office can function as a real champion of the consumer or will simply act as a propaganda arm of the Postal Service.

The Consumer Advocate as of this writing is Thomas W. Chadwick, Room 4920, Postal Service, L'Enfant Plaza West, Washington, D.C. 20260. Chadwick is a mild-mannered man, with horn-rimmed glasses and ten years' experience on Capitol Hill working for the House Post Office and Civil Service Committee, plus seven years with the old Post Office and its successor. "I have two principles of looking at life, or a job," he says. "First, you have to feel that you accomplish something every day. I know a lot of people who have ninety balls in the air all of the time, look busy, but don't really wind up doing anything. It gives me a lot of satisfaction to find a problem and solve it. Second, you have to look at problems as opportunities.

Years ago a boss of mine said, 'when you have a lemon, what you have to do is find a way to make lemonade.' Now of course if the lemon is spoiled, then there is nothing to be done. But otherwise, that's what you have to do."

Chadwick supplements his know-how with a staff of about fifty people. His job is to administer the unit. Matters like personnel or philately are referred to staff specialists.

As for complaints, "On an annual basis, we receive here at Headquarters around 25,000 to 30,000 complaints a year," explains Chadwick. "This may sound like a lot—and in a way it is—but you have to remember that if we make a mistake, for example of one tenth of one percent—that could generate 125,000 complaints a day.

"I've been called a 'professional meddler,'" Chadwick admits. "That is, as the complaints come in, I have to answer them and pass on observations to the operational elements and encourage them to do something about them. We often answer the complaints by phone. Very few form letters are used. When they are, they are restricted to something like the design of an airgram, or a problem of glue, when a form letter actually answers the complaint. Otherwise, they receive individual responses."

In short, Chadwick's group must both soothe feelings and try to get operational action from the people responsible. As he sees it, "The problem in this job, of course, is the conflict between service and efficiency or productivity. I can't very well take the position, for instance, that mail should be delivered to the door instead of a central lobby. So I have to weigh the problem, and if it is reasonable, approach the people here to see if they can do something about it."

Having an Office of Consumer Advocate poses a temptation to the Postal Service to use the office as a public relations gimmick. Whenever charges of deteriorating service arise, out pops the Consumer Advocate. In a June 1973 report Chadwick said that weekly complaints from customers received at Postal Service headquarters had dropped 70 percent since a January 1973 high and that next-day delivery of first-class mail was again at 95 percent. During the ordinary week, Chadwick said he received about 500 complaints, down from 1,009 during the week of January 19. For April of that year, he added, nationally reported complaints from local post offices had dropped 16 percent from the January 1973 level.

This latter statistic is not as encouraging as it may sound; the local post offices might well have handled more complaints themselves. The role of Consumer Advocate presumably should be to prod the post office for better service. Putting forth claims of Postal Service improvement might better come from operating units responsible for whatever improvements may have been made.

The Consumer Advocate would in fact have greater clout if consumers use it as a weapon to make the Postal Service back up its claims of customer satisfaction. In the summer of 1974 I requested a check of delivery of *The New Republic* magazine, against a background of increasing complaints on late delivery and nondelivery of the publication. Chadwick responded, despite his concern over the cost of such a survey. His monitoring showed that indeed delivery was worse, but that it was within the tolerance to be expected. Nothing has been done to improve service, although second-class rate increases march on.

In addition to the three areas of progress discussed above, the Postal Service would cite its investment in bulk-mail facilities and in first-class mail processing equipment as major accomplishments. As we have seen, however, the final word is not in on these programs. The fact that the percent of budget allocated to labor rose from 84.9 percent in fiscal 1972 to 85 percent in fiscal 1973 belies Postal Service claims of ever-increasing productivity per worker. Added to this is the fact that service levels are still below the old Post Office standards, although the price of a first-class stamp has risen from six cents to ten cents and may reach twelve or thirteen cents in 1975. In short, performance in these major spheres casts serious doubts on the validity of the postal corporation concept.

VIII

INNOVATIONS—THE BOARD OF GOVERNORS AND THE POSTAL RATE COMMISSION

Two important new components of the re-organized Postal Service were the Board of Governors and the Postal Rate Commission (PRC). Under the reorganization bill, "the exercise of the power of the Postal Service shall be directed by a Board of Governors composed of eleven members...." The pay is $10,000 per year, plus not more than thirty days at $300 per day for attending board meetings. The board selects the Postmaster General (who is also a board member) and can remove him.

The Postmaster General is the chief executive officer of the Postal Service. Thus, the responsibility for administering the Post Office has been transferred from the hands of Congress into the lap of the Board of Governors. As suggested by the Kappel Commission, Congress also handed over its authority to set postal rates (long a touchy issue) to the new Postal Service, and to a new Postal Rate Commission, a so-called independent body, although it can be overruled by the Board of Governors. This ambiguous delegation of powers created tensions that contributed to the early resignation of the first two chairmen of the PRC.

The Board of Governors as the responsible authority for the Postal Service has taken a good deal of flack for the poor performance of the mail service. Chairman of the Board Kappel, replaced in December 1974 by M. A. Wright, chairman of Exxon, was assertive of his prerogatives in dealing with Congress. In his public appearances before congressional committees, he came on strong as a man who knew what he wanted. A conservative dresser with gray close-cut hair and glasses with a built-in hearing aid, he carried a full briefcase and seemed to be working as hard as or harder than ever before, serving on various charitable organizations as well as on the Postal Service board.

Kappen considered his two biggest problems to be the Office of Management and Budget, which has interfered with the Postal Service budget, and the Congress. Although he felt that the 1970 legislation may have been imperfect, in his opinion it was sufficient to do the job if the members of Congress would leave the bill alone. As Kappel saw it, Congress should have a self-policing system so that once Congress votes to pass a law, its members cannot spend their time trying to undermine it. He cited H. R. Gross's proposed 1973 bill to give Congress yearly approval over the Postal Service budget as a step in the wrong direction.

Kappel claimed that the postal corporation is making progress, but that the service is too large to run around overnight. In an emphatic statement before the House subcommittee in 1973 he said:

I challenge any member of Congress to want a first-class Postal Service more than do the Board of Governors and the very able Postmaster General. Postal management, with the full support and involvement of the Governors, is working all-out to this end. I believe that great numbers of postal officials and postal workers have this same determination. They deserve every support and opportunity that you can give them. Given your encouragement—at least to the point of accepting the fact that this is a very tough job at best—the prospects for improved postal service are immeasurably greater than they would have been if the Reorganization Act had not been enacted.

In general the Board of Governors operates like the board of directors of any large corporation, with a set of operating procedures for the overview of performance, for major financial and budgetary matters, for long-range planning, for significant capital investment programs, for career development and training programs, for major collective bargaining developments, and so forth. Its single most important function, in Kappel's view, was the selection of the Postmaster General, to whom the board delegates "authority to exercise the powers of the Postal Service so that he may carry out his responsibilities. . . ." Former President Nixon, before taking over the office of President, and prior to the postal reorganization, consulted Kappel on what kind of man he should select as his Postmaster General. Kappel advised Nixon to find someone with broad experience in running a large corporation with a big labor force, and who wasn't a lawyer—lawyers being notoriously low, in Kappel's view, in management ability.

Winton Blount, the man lawyer Nixon subsequently selected, filled at least part of the bill. He was, however, a politician as well as a businessman, which led him to straddle the fence on postal reorganization. Blount did, however, deserve Kappel's approbation for the way he finally squared off with Congress to demonstrate that the reorganization in 1970 was not a fiction. Blount was replaced by Klassen on January 1, 1972, who gave the Postal Service, in Kappel's words, "the strong management leadership that it must have to succeed." Bailar's tenure is yet too brief to pass judgment.

Kappel felt that Klassen's $60,000 salary and the salary of the deputy ($57,500 with the job unfilled at this writing) were false economies and that the way to build up a broad depth of managerial talent was to raise the salary levels of the Postal Service, a proposition that Congress has so far resisted, given its embarrassment over handling federal pay scales. Kappel, however, was relentless on this point. As he saw it, "The one most important thing that the Congress can do to improve postal service in this country is to remove the existing limit on executive salaries." The problem here, as noted earlier, is that lifting the salary lid in one area of government sets off a reaction throughout the entire system. Neither the Congress nor the taxpayers are presently willing to accept the consequences of such a move.

Reinforcing his efforts to impress on Congress the proper attitude toward the Postal Service, Mr. Kappel said, at the hearings before Representative James Hanley's (D.,

N.Y.) Post Office and Civil Service Subcommittee on May 2, 1973:

> It would be a public service of major propor-
> tions, and perhaps an act of political statesman-
> ship as well, if you would join the Board of
> Governors and Mr. Klassen and his people in
> their dedication of making postal reform suc-
> ceed. It is a tremendous undertaking that we are
> engaged in—to give the public the kind of service
> that it can be proud of at acceptable levels of
> cost and to create satisfying working conditions
> and rewarding career opportunities for all postal
> employees. If we work together at it as respon-
> sible citizens, we can make a real contribution to
> this country and we might accomplish some-
> thing unique in Washington bureaucracy while
> we're at it. I urge your objective and construc-
> tive support.

Congress for its part is not certain that the Board of Governors is as public-service oriented as Kappel claimed. In the view of Representative Udall, the Board of Gover-nors is too homogeneous, representing only a business point of view. The nine board members listed in the December 1973 annual report included a rancher, three industrialists, a banker, a retired educator, and a dentist/ real-estate developer, plus Kappel and Klassen. Udall feels that given the importance of labor to the Postal Service it might be beneficial to have the postal workers represented on the board. In response, Kappel, while agreeing that this idea may have merit, believed that appointments to the board should not represent a particular constituency. Kappel's views in this matter, however, are academic, since the appointment of the governors is in the hands of the President, and the chairman of the Board of Governors, who is not consulted, learns about them from the newspaper like everyone else.

Both Senators McGee and Fong, incidentally, have reportedly gotten friends onto the board.

The presidentially appointed members of the board can include no more than five from the same political party. The fact that the board in general shows little interest in party politics has caused Representative William D. Ford (D., Mich.) to state: "I don't respect the idea that people don't stand up for one party or another."

This lack of political bias on the part of the board has had a mixed effect from the citizen's point of view. Public assets turned over to the Postal Service to launch the government corporation are now very much in the hands of the board, but the board is not really connected to the U.S. Government in a practical way. As before mentioned, Kappel in his official capacity as board chairman did not see the President for over five years. He refused, probably wisely, to work with any other member of the White House staff on postal matters. Thus the board, in a real sense, operates quite outside the White House orbit.

The board's relationship to the OMB is also tenuous, although by budget cutting, the OMB has forced the Postal Service, in the case of third-class (advertising) mail, to impose the full rates faster than the Postal Rate Commission's phasing program called for—much to the outrage of former Postmaster General Day and his Associated Third-Class Mail Users. If the Postal Service Budget is ever balanced, the OMB link would in practical terms be cut. That not being the case, however, the OMB can in effect veto postal rate phasing extension legislation by persuading the president to recommend against approval of the funds.

Beyond political questions, there have been other reservations about the concept of a Board of Governors. In the words of Senator McGee:

> One area of concern . . . is the mechanics of the setup for the operation of the corporation, the board, for example. What burden of continuing responsibility could a part-time board have in this operation more than having an open meeting and getting the appointment or designation? Aren't we just retreating from one system where responsibility was rather loosely laid to another system where it is still rather loosely reposed?

The Senator seemed to have a point. The monthly meetings are held in what seems excessive secrecy, and the reports that issue from these gatherings, as we shall shortly see, are remarkably uninformative.

The Postal Rate Commission is another controversial result of the Reorganization Act. As before mentioned, Kappel in his 1968 report saw the rate-making function working as follows: "The Corporation management would develop rate proposals and forward them to a panel of technically-qualified Postal Rate Commissioners responsible only to the Board of Directors." The actual legislation gave the commission even greater independence. "There is established, as an independent establishment of the executive branch . . . the Postal Rate Commission. . . ." In practice, rate recommendations are sent by the Postal Rate Commission to the Board of Governors of the Postal Service, where they are approved, allowed under protest, or rejected. Recommendations can be modified only on the written unanimous agreement of all board members.

Kappel, a believer in the principle of regulation in the public interest, was a staunch defender of the PRC. "There is no way to work through an already established commission," he responded to a question of the writer's about why a regulatory agency could not have been conceived as part of the nation's communications network under the Federal Communications Commission. The PRC, however, is not quite the tame regulatory agency that Kappel may have been aiming for.

If Caesar's wife had been obliged to work for the U.S. Government, her best bet to preserve her purity would have been to get a job with the Postal Rate Commission. Set up by the 1970 postal reorganization legislation, the commission is the epitome of the no-gifts, no-dealing-with-influence-peddlers, no-nonsense approach. Such virtue, however, takes its toll in the effectiveness of the PRC.

The idea of regulation of natural monopolies came to the fore during the administration of Theodore Roosevelt. It arose in response to the need to protect the citizens and the government itself from the predatory giants let loose on the land—the burgeoning oil, gas, electric, railroad, and transportation and communications monopolies that prospered according to the principle of unrestricted competition in a free economy amid the seemingly bound-less resources of the United States. The Samuel Insulls are long gone, and their modern counterparts have chafed at the lack of opportunity to receive more than 15 percent profit on their services. Such public resources, as water power and natural gas, somehow are thought to be the property of the first fellow to stake a claim. To be sure, these champions of free enterprise have never balked at going back to the regulators each year to get increases in the price for their services to assure that their profits, as in the case of Western Union, don't fall below 14 percent before taxes. In a jungle of regulations, the regulated parts of the American economy fare very well indeed, since built into their vow to eschew exaggerated profits is a guarantee that they can't lose money. Not a bad deal in this other-wise uncertain world.

The theory of regulation in the American system is that only "natural" monopolies should be subject to controls. Which activities fall into this category and why is a matter of endless dispute. For example, the regulators ask, don't gas and electric companies really compete, if not, respec-tively, with other gas and electric companies, then with each other? To the consumer, however, much of this com-petition is theoretical. In Washington, D.C., for example, if you don't buy your electricity from Potomac Electric, you are reduced to gas lamps or candles.

On the outer edge of the logic of regulation lie the airlines. After all, if you want to go to New York, there are plenty of ways to get there—train, car, bus, bicycle. The fixed fares on air travel appear to many to be rigged against the consumer, and the vitality of any real competition in the airlines is vitiated by their ownership by the large banks (who make their buck, regulation or no regulation, through such devices as forcing their captive carriers to lease airplanes at high interest rates to the banks instead of buying their aircraft for cash).

One of the critical factors in the postal reorganization was the decision to consider the Postal Service as a public utility. The larger issue of whether public utilities, like the telephone, gas, and electric companies, are doing a good job for the consumer was conveniently bypassed. The Post Office was simply designated as a utility by the Kappel report, whether it qualified or not.

Within the PRC, there is a feeling that regulation is basically a bad idea, that the Postal Service is what it says it is, and that any interference with management prerogatives should be minimal—more perhaps than the Postal Service finds acceptable but less than a consumer or the public interest might desire.

Despite this antiregulatory bias, the PRC has gradually grown more ambitious. In its first rate case on June 5, 1972, it presented its position as follows:

> The beginning of the Commission's inquiry is to determine how much revenue the Postal Service needs. The Postal Service has argued that the Commission has no jurisdiction to review the Service's estimates of total costs and revenues. Contrary to the Service's position, however, the Act specifically entitles the Governors to this Commission's independent judgment whether these estimates accord with the statutory policies.

106

William J. Crowley, a former executive of the Illinois Gas Company, and the first chairman of the PRC, was a strong advocate of the commission's rights. As in the case with other federal regulatory agency heads, Crowley was in fact independent, being responsible directly to the President, who, even on clear days, was not likely to see as far as the PRC. The presidential eyesight improved remarkably, however, whenever something happened that upset the serenity of his important constituents, like big business. Miles Kirkpatrick, former chairman of the Federal Trade Commission, for example, left in the middle of his eight-year term, because the FTC became too interested in advertising claims, questioning the statements of such giants as ITT and the patent medicine lobby.

Outside pressures on the PRC are minimal. The visible lobbies, like the Magazine Publishers Association, the religious publications, and the nonprofit, tax-free foundations, have little clout with the commission. The June 5, 1972, rate hearing report was a model of laying it on the line as to the inequities of certain postal rates, and the classifications hearings that started in 1973 were subject to comparatively little important political pressure. The decisions on these matters move millions of dollars to special-business interests or to the public, but large as the sums are, the political impact of classification questions is slight as opposed to their economic repercussions.

Since Mr. Crowley saw his mandate to be independent as a real one, disharmony was perhaps inevitable between the Postal Service and the PRC. While the commission was still located in the main post office building before acquiring its own offices in downtown Washington, Mr. Crowley would not use the elevators for fear of consorting with Postal Service officials. His concern for the appearance of propriety spread even to food: he refused to dine in the basement cafeteria. While such actions might seem excessive, they were part of a serious effort to assert the independence of the PRC from the monster Post Office.

Kappel and the Postal Service were opposed to review of the service's budget by the PRC. As Kappel put it, "I would not extend the PRC's authority. Let's not spread that disease into the Postal Service." Kappel felt that agitation on the PRC's part for more authority reflected the lack of enough work to do when rate or classification cases weren't being heard.

After less than two years on the job, Crowley abruptly resigned—or as abruptly as he could. He first submitted his resignation in February 1973, and then again in April. Upon getting no word from the President, he packed up and went back to Illinois. He finally got his resignation "with regret" on May 1, 1973. Kappel the next day said that he was sorry to see Crowley go, but had had no "prior knowledge" of his departure.

Ostensibly the reason for Crowley's resignation was over the reclassification hearings, then under way, in which he felt the Postal Service was not participating as fully as it should. The PRC wanted to examine the entire classification system, with the view of rationalizing and simplifying it. In a *Wall Street Journal* article dealing with postal reclassification, Crowley's successor, Chairman John L. Ryan, said that the present classification system is "oriented to giving special rates to special customer groups" and that this may have become anachronistic. He said that the commission did not intend to limit itself "to being a mere umpire, calling balls and strikes only on the proposals of parties who can afford to participate actively in the hearings." The estimated cost for full intervention in a rate or classification case, complete with qualified lawyer, is at least $100,000, which helps to explain why the average citizen's postal interests, centering around the cost of a first-class stamp, are not always easily represented.

To meet the problem of consumer participation, the PRC in fact hired a lawyer to represent the general public. Predictably enough, this representative urged the lowering of first-class rates, stating that this would avoid "requiring mailers receiving monopoly service to support classes receiving competitive service, since most first-class mail is subject to the Postal Service monopoly and the first-class mailers are thus ... captives of the system." To make up for this revenue loss to the Postal Service, he proposed higher rates for the other classes of mail.

As commission chairman, Mr. Crowley had set an interesting example. He had kept his staff small—around fifty, about half of what he was allowed—came to work at 7:30 A.M. and left at 6 P.M. He was a lawyer and a tax accountant. His office was filled with charts and graphs on Postal Service performance, and his was the only office of a commission chairman in Washington without a carpet on the floor.

Mr. Ryan succeeded Crowley in August 1973, only to resign two months later, apparently convinced that his replacement was at hand. The third chairman, Fred Rhodes, however, was not on board until January 1974. This rapid turnover in chairmen in part prompted hearings in January 1974 by Representative Hanley's subcommittee on the operation and organization of the PRC. Further embarrassment to the PRC was occasioned in December 1974 when Mr. Rhodes resigned to benefit from a federal pension increase. A temporary chairman was then appointed.

Exactly what the PRC can or will do is still an open question. The 1974 Hanley hearings did, however, shed light on its attitudes and how it works. In that respect, the testimony of former Chairman John Ryan, safely out of the ring, was surprisingly forthright by the standards of subcommittee hearings. Ryan took an extremely conservative view regarding the PRC's authority, contrary to his previous position that the commission was more than an umpire calling balls and strikes. "It appears to be the impression of many people, that, by the application of skill, knowledge and hard work, the Postal Rate Commission can somehow hold down postal rates and improve service. It cannot. It cannot even apply much independent judgment as to what individual rates should be and, in my opinion, should not have much powers beyond the current extent." He continued that "it can, and I believe has already, made some imaginative contributions in the matter of mail classification, but in the matter of rates and service, it is limited by real circumstances it cannot and should not be able to control."

And if this were not enough, Commissioner Ryan exposed his personal philosophy on the whole rate-making idea, bringing up the contradiction between a natural monopoly (like utilities) and a statutory monopoly, like the Postal Service. In the latter case, as far as postal rates are concerned, he saw only four choices: (1) "abandon the breakeven concept of the Postal Reorganization Act which will throw much of any increase in expense on the backs of the taxpayers;

(2) continue as we are going, which will increasingly load a larger burden on the first-class mailers; (3) put all of the Postal Service product lines under statutory monopoly protection; (4) remove the monopoly protection from letter mail and allow competition across the board, at the same time freeing the Postal Service itself from monopoly requirements." Expressing his personal priorities, Commissioner Ryan went on to say that "the last choice is so persuasive that it is really the only one. It will reduce mailing costs to the general mailer and improve service to everyone."

The Hanley subcommittee was not anxious to hear either of these statements. Former Postmaster General Day's response on Ryan's limited theory of Rate Commission power was blunt. "It strains common sense to assume Congress created an independent Commission with five Presidential appointees and a staff of high-level specialists merely to perform this limited tinkering function." Day pointed up the commission's responsibility to see that postal rates are "reasonable, fair and equitable. The Commission in fact has a broad and unique role to play in determining the reasonableness of the rate for each class and subclass. The Commission does not by any means have to give the Postal Service the full amount of new revenue it asks for in the form of higher rates."

On the heretical position that the postal monopoly should be abandoned altogether, Representative Hanley asked the then new PRC Chairman Rhodes about the commission's views on the repeal of the Private Express statutes, which since 1972 had given the government the exclusive right to carry letters. The commissioner ducked. Hanley then queried the other commissioners. "Has this issue ever been the subject of deliberation with the Rate Commission?" Commissioner Saponaro replied, "No, sir. No, it hasn't."

In view of the almost institutionalized unresponsiveness of the Postal Service's Board of Governors to outside forces, the more the PRC can pressure better service and lower costs out of the Postal Service through its recommendations on rates and classifications, the better it is likely to be for the consumer. Mr. Rhodes felt that the PRC is now the congressional surrogate on the fairness and reasonableness of rates. In practice, however, this means setting rates only in terms of costs with no meaningful consideration of social, cultural, or educational consequences. He would also have liked to see questions of rates and classifications aired, giving the public as well as the Postal Service a better understanding of these issues and concerns.

The PRC has received extensive congressional criticism because of the months and years spent on the rate and classifications hearings. These hearings are, however, necessarily complex, with hundreds of interveners and many thousands of pages of testimony. Given the intricacies involved, the resulting mountains of fine print are not superfluous. For example, should there be a lower rate on postcards along with slower service? Should first-class letters already presorted by ZIP code, or into even finer groupings, be allowed a lower rate, or would such a rate deprive the Postal Service of so much revenue that it would delay its own investment in mechanization?

Criticism of the PRC's role in rate-making continues along the grounds that rates are still a political matter and that therefore the Congress must still play a direct role.

Postal rates do profoundly affect the business, social, and educational welfare of the nation. Removing the management of the mails to a disinterested Board of Governors and allowing rates to be set by technicians may be an exceptional, and largely unforeseen, price to pay for the 1970 Postal Reorganization Act.

IX

POSTAL PERFORMANCE—OUTCRIES FROM CONGRESS

On August 28, 1972, Postmaster General Klassen announced at a news conference that thanks to his economy measures, it would not be necessary to raise first-class mail rates in 1973. The economies Klassen cited were mainly reduction in staff. No first-class postage rise in 1973 was one of the last pieces of good news to come out of the Postal Service.

The draconian reduction in postal workers effected in 1972-73 was bound to take its toll on the movement of the mails. Thus it did not go by unnoticed, as Klassen apparently had expected. In the "Outlook" section of the Washington *Post* of November 26, 1972, Robert J. Samuelson, a staff writer, wrote a long and thoughtful piece entitled "Why the Mail Is a Mess." He attributed the fundamental problem of the Postal Service to the deterioration of the "three solid pillars" which were still holding up the old Post Office at the end of World War II: (1) cheap

115

labor, (2) adequate passenger train network, and (3) an "uncritical political climate" that allowed large postal deficits to pass unchallenged. After reviewing the modernization plans and Klassen's confidence in management magic, Samuelson concluded that "the Postal Service is not at all assured of ultimate success." The impending Christmas mail rush might tell the story.

On the same day a featured article appeared in the business section of *The New York Times* entitled "Postal Critics Alive and Kicking." Despite the headline, the survey showed that dissatisfaction with the mails was limited, and that aside from certain problem areas, service was considered acceptable. "I see no essential difference in service. We feel it's a little too early for that," said John Makinen, general director of the printing and purchasing department of the John Hancock Mutual Life Insurance Company. After all, the Postal Service with its new management philosophy had been in operation for only sixteen months.

On January 2, 1973, Mike Causey in his "Federal Diary" column in the Washington *Post,* reported that "Postal Service Conquers Christmas." According to Causey, "Despite dark predictions of a pre-Christmas collapse, the U.S. Postal Service is still with us, head held high." He went on, however, to cite the "serious doubts" of certain union officials that the Postal Service figures were accurate. No one yet knew about the 3,475 sacks of mail in Charleston, West Virginia, that had remained unprocessed over the holidays.

On January 5, 1973, the Postmaster General issued an annual report for the fiscal year 1972 announcing that the Postal Service had reduced its losses some 14 percent to

$175,435,000. As mentioned earlier, the figure did not take into account the $1.4-billion subsidy which has traditionally been considered part of the cost of mail service and hence part of the deficit.

Klassen further claimed that first-class mail service, which affects the average citizen most, had achieved a 94 percent next-day delivery average, decreasing delivery time from 1.7 to 1.6 days. The kindest thing to be said of this statistic is that it is meaningless, but there is good reason to be less indulgent. Representative H. R. Gross, on January 18, 1973, entered a rejoinder in the *Congressional Record* based on a Government Accounting Office survey he had requested. This survey showed that the service had in fact been "adversely affected by economy measures taken by the Postal Service," and was worse than it had been in the latter half of fiscal year 1969. Gross also disclosed that in arriving at the reduced figures the Postal Service had neglected to count the time it takes for first-class mail to be collected, transported, prepared for postmarking, sorted for delivery by carriers, or delivered. Hence the new statistics bore almost no relation to the actual service experienced by the customers.

By February all the facts about the Christmas mail situation were in, and on the eighteenth of that month *The New York Times* ran a front-page article: "A Slowing of Mail Delivery Conceded by Postal Chief." The cat was out of the bag and soon every member of Congress and most citizens in the country knew about the slowdown—if not breakdown—of the Postal Service. The Senate Post Office-Civil Service Committee, at the urging of Senator Randolph, decided to hold investigations of the mail service.

On the House side, the Hanley subcommittee decided to follow suit, bringing the controversy over the performance of the Postal Service during its first twenty months under the Reorganization Act into full public view.

Senator McGee opened the hearings on March 7, 1973. The first scheduled witness was the Postmaster General himself, who played to a standing-room-only crowd, including wall-to-wall lobbyists and a visiting band of high school students. Even television was on hand, highlighting the new surge of interest in Post Office affairs. There were too many reporters for the available seats.

Postmaster General Klassen, an awkward speaker at best, was ill equipped for this type of carnival public performance. Handkerchief in hand, he had begun to mop his brow, even before the show was on the road.

"I am more convinced than ever that reorganization can and will provide more efficient postal service." Klassen read from his prepared statement, going on to enumerate his main accomplishments as steward of the Postal Service. Klassen announced that the mail service was "somewhat better" than on July 1, 1971, when the Postal Service was established. Like many of Klassen's claims, this was never substantiated during this or subsequent hearings. He relied mainly on his own flawed annual report to show progress. The situation was not helped by the fact that Klassen was facing a group of Senators who had been treated to a growing mountain of complaints about the deterioration of the service. Guilt feelings about turning over their responsibilities on postal affairs to the government corporation may have been another factor that motivated Senators to use the hearings

118

to impress their concern about the mails on the folks back home.

The Postmaster General's testimony at first proceeded tamely and dully enough. This was Klassen's first starring appearance at such a hearing, and he and his staff, ignoring practical considerations, produced a ponderous forty-eight-page statement which Klassen unfortunately decided to read in full. McGee suggested that the testimony simply be inserted into the record and key points discussed, but Klassen would have none of it. The immediate result of this maneuver was to send the high school students into retreat.

The line of Klassen's testimony was a fleshing out of the annual report—about as enlightening as the International Telephone and Telegraph Annual Report would be on the subject of ITT's activities in Chile with the CIA. Klassen's strategy was to admit minor service difficulties and claim major organizational accomplishments. He stated that the federal payment was down almost $700 million, half of the highest year, and that there had been no first-class postage increase. The reason for this flowed from the next statement, that there were now 64,000 fewer employees, down to 680,000. In 1972 Klassen said that the Postal Service spent $393 million on the modernization program, compared to only $130 million in the whole period from 1959 to 1971. New mail-processing plants were springing up like pickle factories, and some 5,000 post offices were being upgraded. One of the simplistic charts attached to his testimony showed the "working conditions improvement program," or percentage of employees in adequate working environments. This was claimed to be 21 percent in 1972, 45 percent in 1973, 65 percent in 1974, and 95 percent in 1975. (Why the Postal Service decided there was no hope for the other 5 percent was not stated.) None of these statistics—some of them bogus—were, of course, to the point.

The first questions from Senator McGee were mild enough and focused on delays in delivery, a common enough experience for most of us. Klassen conceded that to avoid a first-class postal rate increase, say to ten cents from eight cents, a $1.2-billion matter, he had concentrated on cutting costs. But he was slow to acknowledge the real and obvious delays. Instead, he retreated to assertions that through his program of placing more management responsibility on local managers, there would in the future be a better standard of balancing between service and cost. His goal was a 93-95 percent one-day delivery service in metropolitan areas. He said the average time for first-class delivery before postal reorganization was 1.4 days, and that this had been lowered under his administration to 1.2 days during the last quarter of 1972, a figure properly greeted with skepticism. (In fact, according to Robert Kessler of the Washington *Post* [June 10, 1974] the policy under Blount in 1969 was not to process first-class mail from distant points except in the daytime to avoid overtime pay costs.)

In the developing interchange between the Postmaster General and the committee members, McGee emphasized that what he wanted to get at was the whys of the problem. He was concerned that there might be something endemic to the Postal Service that caused delivery problems and feared that the progress reported by Klassen might come from bad or inaccurate or loaded reporting.

Klassen responded by saying that the problem in all organizations was telling the boss what he wanted to hear. His familiar solution was to get the responsibility down to the lowest feasible level, so that local managers would run the system and would be responsible for the success and failure of their own district. Klassen hoped to get away from the *Postal Manual* approach to problems and instead start those local managers exercising informed judgment.

A friend in court for Klassen was Senator Fong, who ostensibly joined the complainers about poor mail service (for the newsletter to the folks back on Oahu) but who had actually been loaded by prehearing briefings and asked only friendly questions. The hand of the Postal Service was clearly in evidence as Senator Fong displayed information he was not likely to have gotten any other way. He wanted to compare investment per employee in the Postal Service ($2,090 in 1973) to the American Telephone & Telegraph ($35,000). This, of course, had been one of the basic messages in the Kappel report. The Postmaster General responded on signal by noting that more investment would be needed to do the job right, that there was some resistance to change among the employees, and that more equipment was being bought and under design. He also observed somewhat defensively that "all the bad service in this country is not in the Postal Service."

The next questioner, in a voice shaking with rage, was Senator Randolph, who asked Chairman McGee for time.

The cause behind Randolph's apoplectic state was fairly typical of the Postal Service's disregard for public and congressional relations. "According to CBS radio this morning,"

121

blustered Randolph, "you made a statement that you didn't have any concern about these hearings because 'I really don't give a damn what the politicians say about mail service.' "

There was a brief silence in the room while Randolph glowered at Klassen. "I said, you indicated that you 'didn't give a damn' what politicians said," the Senator continued. "Is that a correct quote?"

A thoroughly flustered Klassen replied: "I don't believe so." (In checking the story, a CBS reporter quoted the Postmaster General as saying: "I'm not going up with my hand out for more money, so I don't really give a damn what the politicians say.") Then Klassen added, painfully, "If some retraction should be made, Senator, I'll do it."

But by now the committee was out for blood. The whole litany of problems facing the service were brought up—the right-to-strike problem, competition from UPS, comparability salary levels, the bulk mailing facilities. In reply to charges by Senator Ernest F. Hollings (D., S.C.) that the Postal Service had deteriorated even further since the reorganization, Klassen, not his own best witness, insisted that the deterioration had long ago set in. This put Klassen in the ambiguous position of saying that the reorganization was fine and workable, while conceding that the Postal Service wasn't working as it should.

Hollings was not to be placated. "The old Post Office really wasn't so bad," he argued. "We wanted to improve the system, and did not want to appoint postmasters. We got that kind of politics out. The trouble is that the mail is not coming through. Banks are afraid to use the mail. Congress has put 10 billion at your disposal to improve the Post

122

Office. Your statement that we should be patient doesn't go well. I see in all this a weakness of management and I wonder about the competence of your team. I had misgivings about the act to begin with. The service is deteriorating, and your adversary attitude toward the Congress is poor."

Now it was former Senator William B. Saxbe's (R., Ohio) turn to carry the ball. "A certain percentage of complaints is expected," he said. "There has been, however, an ever increasing number of complaints being registered with Congressional offices. The interesting aspects about these complaints is that they are not from any one particular segment of our society. No. They arrive from all types of individuals in different parts of the country. But there is one aspect that gives them a type of unity. They all complain that the mail service is deteriorating at a noticeable and rapid rate."

Senator Frank E. Moss (D., Utah) chimed in to report that he had received more complaints about the "deplorable state of the mails" in the last six months than at any comparable period since he had come to the Senate in 1959. He added caustically, "The complaints have become so numerous that I've begun to wonder how many other protests I have *not* received because they have been delayed somewhere in the mails." Moss had no doubt about where to lay the blame: "I believe it is appropriate that we are beginning with a hard look at the top management, for it appears that most of the current problems originate in the upper executive echelons." He zeroed in on the following "imperative points."

- At a time when deteriorating service is blamed

on a "cost crunch," how can management justify the hiring of more than 1,800 executives at salaries greater than $15,000 a year?

- How can management justify salaries of more than $42,000 a year for at least 20 top postal officials?
- Was it wise to reduce the number of postal employees by 65,000 during a period when mail volume increased by 2 billion pieces?
- Does it make sense for new inexperienced executives in Washington to impose rigid untried management techniques on experienced employees in the field?

"There may be problems," Moss persisted, "in the postal service aside from mismanagement in Washington, but from all the information I have been able to obtain, the main problems lie at the top. I know, for example, that many of the veteran postal employees in Utah have felt themselves shackled by directives emanating from Washington. Postmaster General Klassen should be complimented for bringing some 85 district managers to Washington last month in order to solicit their views on how the postal service should be run. These men represent a wealth of experience, and I am sure that the Postmaster General found their suggestions valuable. I only wish that he had begun to listen to his employees in the field a bit sooner. If he had, the U.S. Postal Service would not have deteriorated to the deplorable state in which we now find it."

Even the charitable Senator Fong had this to say about

the Postal Service's performance: "I must also point out that many of the letters I received contained high praise for the postal employees with whom the correspondents had personal contact. The criticism rather focuses on the 'new system' established for mail flow and the higher postage rates postal patrons are required to pay with no observable improvement in service."

As the hearing progressed it became increasingly evident where public sentiment lay. According to Senator Alan Cranston (D., Calif.), "One telling index to the utter failure of a product or an endeavor is the number of jokes it generates." Cranston, who had received over five thousand complaints within the past year about the mail service, found that no laughing matter. "First there were Edsel jokes. These gave way to TFX and F-111 jokes. Now postal service jokes have become a national pastime." The Senator went on to enumerate a few.

"While the fighting in Vietnam was going on full fury, for example, people were saying: 'Let's turn the war over to the Postal Corporation: they may not end it, but they'll sure slow it down!' Another commentary, according to Cranston was: 'Smash the Mafia—mail it parcel post!' And the following one-liner attributed to Miriam Ottenberg of the Washington *Star-News* was proposed to adorn the Christmas stamp: 'O Lord, Deliver Me.' "

According to Cranston the following factors were responsible for the postal department's ills:

- a "totally unrealistic" hiring freeze
- a "top-heavy" administration
- forced early retirement of qualified personnel

125

- attempts to automate mail handling with "untested systems"
- reduction of mail service

Another critic of the mail service was Senator Jacob K. Javits (R., N.Y.). Goaded on by his large and vocal constituency he stated: "I have tried to understand the rising costs of the various classifications of the mail, but I cannot justify rising costs and deterioration of mail services at the same time." Javits urged a thorough review of postal functions and procedures.

"Impatience is natural," countered the beleaguered Klassen, "but in truth it is premature."

The Postmaster General was finally forced to retreat under fire, having antagonized Senators who, treated with more tact, might have viewed him more kindly. Klassen seemed ill prepared in the first session of the hearings both to present and to rebut arguments, and his entourage of senior Postal Service officials, many with bulging briefcases, added to the impression that the Postmaster General's knowledge of postal affairs was one layer deep. Like most business leaders, Klassen was used to dealing with subordinates, and receiving verbal abuse from the Senators was probably a new experience. If challenged on a point, he would simply repeat his answer louder, like the American tourist who is convinced that the funny-looking native can understand English if the volume is loud enough.

The subsequent House hearings reinforced the call for more emphasis on service. They were followed up by hearings in various cities around the country. This, then, was the background for the legislative lurch in the

Congress to keep a rein on the post office. Congress wanted to make certain, however, that public blame for the further deterioration in the service, and above all the responsibility for the outcome of the Postal Service's negotiations with the labor unions, would point straight to Klassen rather than themselves. Over seventy bills were introduced in the House in the spring of 1973 to get back budget and other authority for Congress. "We in Congress are very concerned with the phenomenal increase in executive power over the past few years," Representative Hanley said on March 29.

None of the proposed measures became law.

X

STAMPING OUT MAGAZINES—
MYTHS AND REALITIES

Magazines and newspapers have enjoyed low postal rates since the earliest days of the Republic. The attraction of being a postmaster for Benjamin Franklin was that it allowed him to peddle his paper more cheaply and efficiently. The tradition of low rates meant that the newspapers flourished as the nation moved West. Papers filled with government information were often mailed free, by frank, by the local Congressman. Thus the romance between Congress and the press was based on mutual advantage. And so it was that the second-class rates were set very low compared to first-class letters, and despite the long years of high postal deficits, have stayed that way. Until recently.

The Postal Reorganization Act of 1970, while promising greater efficiency and cost reduction, carried with it the implicit threat of higher second-class rates. As noted earlier, each class of mail was to pay its attributable costs.

Rate hikes were generally anticipated in the magazine industry, but it was assumed that increases would be modest and would be phased over a comfortably long period of time. Alternatively, the new mechanized Postal Service might actually succeed in delivering the mail faster and cheaper, relieving the necessity for higher second-class rates. There was also the comforting preamble of the act in regard to postal policy. "The Postal Service shall have as its basic function the obligation to provide postal service to bind the Nation together through the personal, educational, literary and business correspondence of the people." Newspapers and magazines felt that they provided an important part of this binding glue, and thus would continue to receive special consideration in terms of the historic second-class subsidy, i.e., the difference between what the Post Office thought it cost to deliver a magazine and the amount charged in postage.

The Postal Service's estimate of the cost of the second-class subsidy is (perhaps deliberately) high. According to the 1972 Postal Service Annual Report, "revenue foregone" on second-class mail was $244.8 million. The Postal Service maintains, however, that the actual subsidy was twice that, because second-class only paid for attributable costs. This charge exaggerates the size of the subsidy, however, because second-class now pays 29 percent of the overhead costs.

There were 9.466 billion pieces of second-class mail sent in 1972, of which regular-rate magazines made up 3.485 billion, or 36.8 percent. If the real second-class subsidy was indeed $488 million instead of $244 million, then regular-rate magazines received $179,604,000 worth of

130

aid. According to the Magazine Publishers Association (MPA), forty-two of its members have 70 percent of the total magazine circulation, which means that these magazines in 1972 received a combined subsidy of $125 million, leaving the balance to be shared by the rest (approximately ten thousand magazines). With this kind of money at stake, it is no wonder that second-class publications, and especially magazines (since less than 6 percent of newspapers are sent by mail), leap into the fray at any prospect of losing this tradition-approved, highly favorable mailing rate.

On February 1, 1971, the Postal Service proposed to the Postal Rate Commission that second-class postage rates be raised about 130 percent over a five-year period to meet the requirement of the law that each class of mail pay for itself. At that time I was a member of the MPA postal committee, and I can assure you that the effect of that announcement was dramatic.

The MPA immediately set to work either to cut back the increase to no more than 5 or 6 percent per year or, at least, to extend the phasing period from the five years provided by the law to at least ten years. If either of these goals could be achieved, there was a chance that additional legislation could be secured during the interim to head off the worst economic effects.

Since the MPA dues are determined by gross dollar volume of the members, it was natural that *Reader's Digest* and Time, Inc., dominate the play and make the decisions. The economics for a publication with mass circulation and those with small circulations are vastly different, however, and I resigned from the MPA on behalf of *The New*

131

Republic to represent better those smaller interests. To this end I helped form the Committee for the Diversity of the Press (CDP), composed of a dozen or so (and now exceeding forty members) other publications with small circulations and tight budgets, through which to present our mutual case during the hearings before the Congress in 1972, 1973, and again in 1975.

Life magazine responded to the postal rate proposals in an editorial in 1971 which was reproduced and disseminated widely by Andrew Heiskell, chairman of the board of Time, Inc. Heiskell claimed a profit of $11 million in 1971 for the Time, Inc., family of magazines—*Time, Life, Sports Illustrated,* and *Fortune,*—while pointing out that under the proposed second-class rates, their postage bill would go up almost $27 million. Competition from TV and newspapers made raising advertising rates per thousand circulation difficult, and higher subscription prices would lead to lower circulation and a downward spiral in advertising revenue.

Interests other than the MPA involved in the second-class rate controversy included the beforementioned American Business Press, the American Newspaper Publishers Association, the beforementioned Committee for the Diversity of the Press, and religious organizations (such as Billy Graham's), nonprofit groups (such as the American Legion), and labor unions (such as the Communication Workers), which have an even lower rate than regular magazines. This latter faction claimed even more impressive percentage rises in its second-class costs on the basis of the new proposals. Increases of 750 percent were discussed with horror, even though the actual postage cost still might

132

be no more than two cents after the phasing. Such was the magic of stressing percentages, which was a universal tactic throughout the hearings.

Unfortunately, the various groups soon fell to squabbling. The ABP was willing to pay somewhat higher postal prices than those proposed by the MPA, ostensibly in the name of better service. The Committee for the Diversity of the Press tried to find a formula that would allow all publications to have a lower rate for a relatively modest base number, say 100,000 later raised to 250,000. This would of course be of proportionately more value to magazines with small circulation than large, but had the advantage of treating all magazines the same, in accordance with their First Amendment rights, an important consideration to Congress. Religious and nonprofit groups basically preferred to pay no postage at all.

Time, Inc., wrote to the CDP members that views contrary to those of the MPA would "drive a wedge" into the magazine front facing Congress, and urged the publications to switch their support to the MPA position. A weighty compilation of arguments and miscellaneous newspaper and magazine editorials opposing the Postal Service's second-class rate increase proposals was attached to this plea. Chapin Carpenter, Jr., director of postal affairs of Time, Inc., and now a vice-president of the MPA, also joined in the letter-writing campaign. On the telephone was Bernard Auer, formerly vice-president for magazines of Time, Inc., threatening that if the CDP did not toe the line, it would be sorry.

The most spirited reply to Time, Inc., came from CDP member Irving Louis Horowitz of *Society* magazine:

"... that you should imagine our side to be based on such thin ice that one letter from *Time* magazine and another from the Magazine Publishers Association should lead us to collapse our efforts is perhaps the saddest comment yet heard."

James Storrow, publisher of *The Nation,* another member of the CDP group, explained the special position of small-circulation magazines to *Time*'s Carpenter as follows:

> Our circulation is, as you know, very small in contrast with yours, and we are not therefore in a position to obtain, proportionately, the advertising income which you receive, and which accounts for the major portion of your revenue. Our income, by contrast, is almost entirely restricted to the sale of subscriptions to our readers. One can quite accurately say that we are in different businesses, so far as our major source of funds is concerned; for us, they derive from the sale of magazines to readers, for you, from the sale of readership to advertisers. I do not say this perjoratively at all, and claim no special virtue in being small; it is a simple statement of fact.

On June 5, 1972, the Postal Rate Commission issued its findings in response to the Postal Service's February 1, 1971, request. In regard to second-class rates, it stated: "Existing rates for regular second-class mail are nominal and have in effect been subsidized by the American tax payer. The second-class mailers must now expect to pay significant rate increases to conform to the provisions of the Act." The PRC's recommendation was a few percentage points less than the figure requested by the Postal Service—an increase of about 127 percent over five years, based on the existing rate levels. This did not include probable augmentations in second-class rates as the Postal Service moved along toward high operating costs.

The PRC decision meant that in July 1972, second-class postage rates would go up about 30 percent, in the case of *The New Republic,* boosting the usual $2,000 per week bill by $600.

The June 19, 1972, issue of *Time,* dated three days before the testimony of Andrew Heiskell before the Udall subcommittee, featured an essay entitled: "Postal Increases: Publish or Perish." The accompanying photo showed the Joseph Pulitzer three-cent stamp, bearing his quote: "Our Republic and its press will rise or fall together." The essay included the following query by Billy Graham, defending the religious press: "Is the Post Office Department, in the name of economy or efficiency or what have you, attempting to tax the exercise of religious freedom?" *Time*'s essayist did not, however, question whether the state should support religion, a logical follow-on. The tone of the article was polemic and it ended on the following sharp note: "The loss of any publication diminishes civilized tradition and shrivels belief in the power of the written word. It is a notion that Jonathan Swift could have constructed: the Post Office is solvent and the press and the readers are deprived."

Heiskell addressed the subcommittee eloquently. "It is a fundamental tenet of our system of government to cherish

135

and encourage a strong, reliable, and free press as indispensable to the survival of democracy," he insisted, going on to explain the roles of the various media in modern society. "If magazines as we know them today were to disappear, the variety and depth of reporting which is critical to a free society would be lost, and I know of no other way to replace it." While making a special case for national magazines of general circulation, Heiskell defended all magazines.

Citing the competition posed by television, Heiskell said that passing along added postal costs to advertisers and subscribers simply wouldn't work. He emphasized novelist Herman Wouk's statement, on behalf of the Authors Guild, that television stations paid very little for the right to use public property, the broadcast channels, on an exclusive basis compared to the second-class postage costs to even a small publication. The rights paid to use channels 2, 4, and 7 in New York, Heiskell said, were well below $100,000 per year.

Mr. Heiskell added: "When our industry supported the idea of the Postal Reorganization Act, we had every reason to believe that the Postal Service would establish reasonable rates taking into account the impact of those rates on our business." He concluded by urging the House subcommittee to consider a ceiling on second-class rate increases.

In the questioning that followed by the members of the committee there was this exchange between feisty H. R. Gross and Heiskell:

> *Mr. Gross:* Mr. Heiskell, were you a member or contributor to that infamous Citizens'

Committee for Postal Reform operated by Mr. Lawrence O'Brien?

Mr. Heiskell: Yes, I was.

Mr. Gross: You were well aware that the Postal Rate Commission was also a part of that postal reform, were you not?

Mr. Heiskell: Yes.

Mr. Gross: Do you now consider that you booby-trapped yourself in supporting that legislation?

Mr. Heiskell: Yes. . . .

On July 25 James Milholland, chairman of the American Business Press (ABP), appeared before the committee, accompanied by general counsel Saltzstein. Milholland's testimony, which was largely devoted to poking holes in the testimony of Mr. Heiskell, illustrates the wide difference of opinion in the magazine business that poses serious problems for legislators bent on finding equitable solutions. The ABP chairman quoted approvingly the testimony of Ed Livermore, president of the National Newspaper Association, representing 5,700 weekly newspapers and 850 small dailies.

Our basic position in summary is, before we come here to ask for Congressional action, we would first like to see that the USPS and the Rate Commission have a reasonable time to function and improve the service. We feel that the present system is the only hope that our members have for the realization of improved mail service.

As for *Time*'s argument that postal increases would wipe out profits, Milholland riposted:

> ... do they really mean to say that they are not going to raise their subscription prices and their advertising prices to cover whatever the increased postage bill may be? In the business press, we certainly intend to raise our prices to reflect additional postage costs. And our product will have to be good enough to warrant that additional price.

The House hearings ended on August 4. Before they were over Senator Gaylord Nelson (D., Wis.) backed up the CDP position by proposing a bill in the Senate to limit second-class increases on the first 250,000 of any publication's circulation. But there was no legislative action in either the House or the Senate in 1972.

By 1973 the MPA and Time, Inc., had a more dramatic case. *Life* had folded in December 1972. Its demise, claimed management, was due in part to the actual and impending second-class rate increases. Why had no one heeded their cries for postal help? As far back as September 1971, Postmaster General Blount had down-played *Life*'s protests about rates as "pessimistic." *Life* in a letter to Blount had pointed out that its second-class bill was $15.4 million per year, and would rise to $42.5 million in the five-year phasing period. Blount's response was that his "independent appraisers" (Mathematica, Inc., of Bethesda, Maryland) had reported that even with higher rates, the magazines would remain in the mail, and that magazines had supported postal reform, fully aware that rates would increase.

The collapse of *Life* magazine coming within six months of the Postal Rate Commission's decision to boost second-class rates 30 percent in 1972, and then onward and upward through the following years, seemed to be the stroke of a master lobbyist. *Life* had warned that it might be priced out of the market and so it had. Norman Cousins in his syndicated column reported a conversation with Hedley Donovan, *Life*'s editor in chief, about postal rate increases. Donovan had said his biggest problem was to convince government officials that *Life* wasn't crying wolf.

The passing of *Life* was more than the termination of just another magazine. It marked the end of a whole era of exciting picture journalism. Hedley Donovan said that *Life* had lost over $30 million in the past four years. Projections showed that deficits would increase, citing competition from television, special-interest magazines, and expected postal rate increases of up to 170 percent. In the Washington *Post*, December 8, 1973, Haynes Johnson eulogized *Life* as follows: "For millions of Americans its demise was like losing a friend of the family. We are all poorer for its loss."

The fact that *Life* was gone added important fuel to the MPA's fire in the 1973 hearings, and the MPA arguments had an apparently sympathetic hearing in the postal committees of both the House and the Senate. The impact of all special-interest pleadings was blunted to some extent, however, by the Postal Service, which was adamant in following the letter of the reorganization law and keeping Congress out of the rate-making process. Benjamin F. Bailar, then senior assistant postmaster general for administration, made a strong case against the second-class mailers, pointing out that although the major magazines were pleading poverty before the Congress, the story on Madison Avenue was one of continuing, even spectacular, financial success. For newspapers, 1972 had been the best in history, and the year had been a good one for many magazines as well, according to MPA President Kelly. Bailar quoted Kelly to the effect that the "Second Great Revolution in Advertising" had occurred, an event akin to the Second Coming. In Kelly's words: "We in the magazine field look ahead with strong convictions of further growth within the industry." Bailar also emphasized the fact that for magazines in the MPA, second-class postage was only 5 percent of their costs and for newspapers about 2 percent. He asserted that even after the fully phased five-year rates, second-class mailers would be paying only 29 percent of their institutional costs, which still left them in an extremely favored position compared to all other classes of mail.

Bailar's strong presentation was reinforced by the fact that the Postal Service has considerably more clout with Congress in terms of its $12 billion budget and 700,000 employees than any combination of magazine and newspaper groups. Yet the second-class mailers had not yet lost their cause. In the House, Representative Hanley proposed legislation extending the phasing and providing for a lower rate on the first 100,000 copies mailed, while in the Senate, the unlikely team of Edward M. Kennedy (D., Mass.) and Barry Goldwater (R., Ariz.) carried the ball on similar legislation designed to preserve a free choice of publications.

In Goldwater's words: "The plight of the nation's magazines and small town and weekly newspapers is a national scandal." Goldwater feared that thousands of these publications faced extinction without congressional action. The Kennedy-Goldwater bill had three aims: (1) to increase the period of rate increases from five to ten years, (2) to assure the first 250,000 circulation of any publication a reduced rate of no more than two thirds of the otherwise applicable rate, and (3) to provide a system of automatic funding to reimburse the Postal Service for revenues it would lose during the ten-year transition period.

The bill, now entitled the "Educational and Cultural Postal Amendments of 1973," came up for debate on the House floor on July 23. Although there was some misgiving about mounting cost, estimated by some at over $300 million and by others at about $1 billion through 1980, there was little reason to believe it would not pass the House. Whether the Senate would be favorably disposed to such a generous and expensive measure was another matter.

As it turned out, the Congress never voted on the bill but dismissed it on a ruling, a substantial victory for the Postal Service in its campaign to stick with the 1970 Reorganization Act.

To the uninitiated the battle over rates now appeared to be over, but this was far from the case. The special-interest groups soon began to coalesce again, and plans were afoot by the fall of 1973 to go forward with new legislation, the idea being that a series of amendments to the Reorganization Act over a period of time would be the wisest course.

141

At Magazine Day in New York in September 1973, Professor Arthur Schlesinger, Jr., was among the speakers to honor magazines and hail Norman Cousins, who had regained *Saturday Review*, as "publisher of the year." Schlesinger's speech later appeared as testimony for the MPA to the Postal Rate Commission and then in an updated, shortened version in January 31, 1974, in *The Wall Street Journal*.

In this article Mr. Schlesinger goes after the Postal Service hammer and tong on behalf of magazines, denouncing rising second-class postal rates. He argues that "the Founding Fathers did not see the postal system merely as a means of raising revenue for the government or of providing facilities for those seeking private profit. They saw it as fundamental to the success of self-government." Quoting with approval former Postmaster General Day's charge that Postmaster General Klassen had a "break-even obsession," Schlesinger goes on to speculate whether the Postmaster General "had any sense of what the Postal Service historically had been all about or, for that matter, that he had ever heard of Washington, Franklin and Jefferson."

This complaint was orchestrated in issues of the *Reader's Digest* and *Time,* and on February 27, 1974, a long defense by then Senior Assistant Postmaster General Bailar appeared in *The Wall Street Journal*. Bailar pointed out that the requirement to "break even" by 1984 was a matter of law as set forth in the Postal Reorganization Act and not a whim of the Postal Service. As for magazines, there were only two ways to maintain the low rates—by tax-financed appropriations, or by having the other classes of mail pick up the slack. In the first case, Congress had not authorized the funds, and in the second, such action was prohibited by law. "One man's free press," said Bailar, "becomes another man's free ride."

Under the Postal Reorganization Act, rates would rise for magazines but still remain a bargain, in Bailar's view. He demonstrated that second-class rates had gone up little for many years, and that such publications as *Reader's Digest* were still being mailed for a little over two cents. Increased postage costs, he believed, could be recouped by charging slightly more for the product. He also cited magazine figures which showed generally good financial health. While Bailar did not disagree that an independent press was essential for a free people, he wondered "whether a truly free press can long endure in this country if editors and publishers become dependent on government subsidies for the economic vitality of their publications."

Schlesinger came back with the last word, charging that the Postal Service was misinterpreting its mandate under the Reorganization Act, citing Senator Goldwater as his authority, and calling for a return to public subsidy of magazine and newspaper mailing rates.

As it turned out, sentiment was on Schlesinger's side. In May 1974 Senator McGee's bill, S-411, was passed, and a companion measure went through the House that June. The effect of the legislation was to extend second-class rate phasing from five to eight years on regular publications and from ten to sixteen years on nonprofits. The estimated cost for the Postal Service through 1988 was $753.7 million.

The significant point here was that the Postal Service through Postmaster General Klassen and Assistant Postmaster General for Government Relations Norman Halliday lobbied strongly in favor of the measure—a complete reversal of form and against the hard-liners in the Postal Service who want the rates to be set "objectively" by the Postal Rate Commission (approved of course by the Board of Governors). Their anxiety to keep Congress totally out of the rate-making business springs from the fear of a speedy return to the old system where one congressional committee voted for expensive subsidies and another, Appropriations, failed to come up with the money.

The reason behind Klassen's support of the new legislation was that he had finally seen the handwriting on the wall. Labor costs were soaring, the new machines weren't working, and service was on the decline. With postal costs in a runaway situation, Klassen could see that the time had come to abandon the line that the costs of the mail must be borne by the user, not the taxpayer, even though this kind of thinking was consistent with the philosophy of the Postal Reorganization Act. In order to hang on to the Postal Service reins, Klassen would have to shift to the subsidy route. At the MPA convention in Palm Beach, Florida, in October 1974, Klassen called for continuing or even higher postal subsidies. He even stated a "break-even" USPS was "totally unrealistic." His successor, however, is equivocable on this point.

The cause of the second-class mailers was further advanced when Representative Hanley introduced a bill in June 1974 calling for a public service subsidy of up to 20 percent of the Postal Service operating budget. This subsidy would require annual authorization from Congress, "an important vehicle by which it could . . . protect the mail user from subsidizing unjustifiable postal expenditures." In a statement on June 20, 1974, Hanley said that the main thrust of his bill was "to provide for a substantially increased subsidy to the Postal Service in recognition of its broad public service function." He also believed it was unwise to continue with the break-even idea, for "if we continue to follow a hard line on the 'break-even' concept, postage rates will continue to skyrocket and non-economic but important postal services could become a thing of the past."

The trend toward subsidy comes none too soon. Not only have magazines in particular suffered from the new second-class rates but second-class mail volume in absolute numbers is falling each year. There may be a compelling argument for permanently lower, or even free, rates for a fairly low number of any publication's circulation, say the first 25,000. This would, in fact, solve a good deal of the postal cost problems for all but the approximately 180 magazines that have circulations over 100,000 and would maintain the public-interest tradition of a diverse press. In the meantime, as Mr. Milholland predicted, in 1974 *Time* raised its basic subscription price from $14 to $18, and *Newsweek* to $19.50.

The renewed sentiment for long-term subsidies for the nation's most basic communications system is indeed a hopeful sign. Because of it, the future of magazines is brighter than in the days when the "break-even" idea was in ascendency.

XI

ONGOING SQUABBLES —COMPETITION AND CORRUPTION

Ever since the enactment of the Private Express Statutes in 1792, the Post Office has enjoyed a legal monopoly over letter mail. The fact that only the official postman can legally put mail in your mailbox has further helped to solidify Post Office control over the mails.

Since fourth-class parcel post, as a category, has had to pay its way by law in the Post Office, rates have been high enough to allow private competition. Within this category, the United Parcel Service is giving the Postal Service a real run for its money.

In the cases of second- and third-class mail, the development of private competition has been sporadic and slow, mainly because of the low rates involved. The high-cost, high-rate operation of the Postal Service, however, has created renewed interest in this area. With second-class postage headed toward a minimum per piece charge of 3.4 cents by 1978, exclusive of weight charges, and third-class already at 6.3 cents and going higher, the economics of alternate delivery systems may alter dramatically.

The MPA has long experimented with alternative delivery of magazines, using milkmen, for example, as a lever against the Postal Service and its high rates. Higher second-class rates may lead to more volume in this area. Jules Beitler, Executive Director, Metropolitan Route Dealers Association, has emphasized that the critical factor for private operators is sufficient volume. Malcolm Forbes, president of *Forbes* magazine, advertised for a better magazine delivery service in response to the Postal Service second-class rate increases, but so far, no private operator has assembled enough magazines to make such a plan feasible.

Third-class mail is another story, failling somewhere between the success of UPS and the lack of appeal for private operators of second-class mail. The Postal Service claims third-class is one of its most profitable classes. Since it has no priority and can be worked in low-volume periods, it lends itself to efficient use of Post Office plant and labor. If a letter is addressed to a name and address, the Postal Service must handle it by law. But unaddressed circulars can be delivered by anyone. It is through this loophole that Thomas Murray and his Independent Postal Service of America (IPSA) tried to wriggle their way to success.

Unfortunately Murray's propaganda efforts for his service outran the pace of his accomplishments, complicated by underfinancing and the hostility of the Postal Service and the postal unions. Murray set out to do for third-class advertising mail—and in selected metropolitan areas, second-class (mainly magazines)—what UPS had done in

148

the fourth-class field. By the time of the IPSA collapse, Murray's "post offices" were delivering over 100 million pieces of mail per year, small potatoes, true, compared to the 90 billion pieces handled by the Postal Service, but enough, nonetheless, to demonstrate that under certain conditions, independents could break into areas of previous postal monopoly.

IPSA was in effect created by the ZIP code system, which lays out the whole country on a five-digit grid. Concentrating on densely populated areas, which made mail sense, IPSA offered franchises to people, often former postal employees, to handle a ZIP code area. The typical franchise sold for ten cents per capita based on the 1960 census. In Tulsa, Oklahoma, for example, $10,000 was paid for 100,000 potential mail customers. IPSA provided the franchise holder with business contracts with magazines, shopping centers, and others who found the system economical. Sporadic volume made it difficult in most instances, however, for the franchise holder to make a consistent profit. IPSA deliveries were made in plastic bags, attached to the door handle, due to the Postal Service's stranglehold on personal mailboxes.

In January 1973 the U.S. Attorney's office in Oklahoma subpoenaed IPSA's books, but Murray was slow to give a clear picture of what he was doing. Six months after the close of his 1973 fiscal year, investors were still waiting for an annual report. In 1973 IPSA was operating in thirty-two states in a disconnected local network. Plans to set up a national distribution system were dashed when the Internal Revenue Service padlocked Murray's business office in Oklahoma City to recover more than $23,000 in

149

delinquent taxes. The Postal Service also charged Murray and two of his associates with mail fraud in the selling of franchises. All were acquitted in 1974, Murray contending that he was being harassed by both the Postal Service and the postal unions who feared competition.

Many other small firms are currently in the mail delivery business, and if postal rates continue to rise, may provide effective competition in the delivery of certain kinds of mail. Without access to first-class, however, a real alternate to the Postal Service appears remote.

As mentioned above, competition for the parcel service is another matter. According to the Postal Service, the UPS is now handling slightly more than 50 percent of the parcel trade. UPS denies this, saying that the Postal Service isn't counting the books, records, and other smaller packages that move through the third-class and the special fourth-class mails. Nonetheless, UPS is a tough customer, doing over $1 billion worth of business annually. Since its beginning in 1907, it has gradually expanded its coverage to all 48 states of the continental United States.

The UPS is a common carrier by motor vehicle, and also operates as a contract carrier in sixteen metropolitan areas. This is what raises the ire of the Postal Service, which charges that through this contract approach, the UPS can "skim" off the cream of the profitable parcel business in congested areas, leaving the distant and unprofitable deliveries to Broken Snowshoe, Idaho, to the Postal Service. These charges are vehemently denied by such UPS spokesmen as Paul Oberkotter, president, and his voluble vice-president, Charles W. L. Foreman.

One of the marked differences between UPS and the

Postal Service is in their style of operation. UPS works out of its New York headquarters, a gleaming cube of a building perhaps a block square with an atmosphere that is Puritan plain. In contrast to the opulence of Postal Service digs, UPS plays it lean and tough. Its employee safety record is superior to the Postal Service, and the company is owned by the employees.

Some say that on occasion the UPS competition approaches a point of dishonesty. In a 1971 opinion, *Marnell v. United Parcel Service of America, Inc.,* the UPS was fined three times $125,000 in a civil suit for illegally monopolizing parcel business in the San Francisco area at the expense of another private competitor. This decision was, however, reversed later.

UPS has its own complaints, especially that the rates the Postal Service sets by law on fourth-class mail users have been too low. It also fears that with the expensive new bulk-mail facilities, it may be unfairly challenged by the Postal Service. In a Postal Forum address, former Postmaster General Klassen said, "I trust there are postmasters in this audience. We are out to get the [parcel post] business. You call the customers, don't wait for them to come to you."

Senator Randolph tweaked the nose of the Postmaster General in the March 1973 McGee hearings. "What about the United Parcel Service? They now have 55 percent of the parcel business. If I'm wrong about that, please correct me." Klassen replied that the UPS is indeed successful, adding: "That's because it does a better job, provides better service, and has taken over $700 million worth of normal parcel post business. They are making a profit on the same business which we lose on. Our problem is that our facilities are poorly designed for this kind of business; the damage is inexcusable and intolerable." In response to a query by Senator Saxbe, however, Klassen claimed that the Postal Service will simply provide better service, once its new bulk-mail facilities are in operation.

What, then, of the idea of repealing the Private Express Statutes, thus opening first-class mail to private competition? The more that the Postal Service pretends that it is a private company, the more vulnerable it is to arguments that postal costs to the public would be reduced and service improved, certainly in the urban areas, if such competition were introduced.

The Board of Governors of the Postal Service on July 1, 1973, proposed certain new rules on Private Express Statutes, which apparently relaxed them in several small and specific areas, but actually potentially expanded the definition of a "letter." This caused concern that the Postal Service, if it were convenient, might apply the letter definition to any printed matter. The specific exemption for first-class was limited to classes of corporate mail that are "so urgent as to require delivery within 12 hours or by the start of the next business day." This would apply only to mail sent between various offices of a single company and to data-processing communications, such as credit and payroll information.

In the hearings in the fall of 1973, Representative Hanley concluded that the Postal Service had too much latitude on the definition of the Private Express Statutes and amendments were included in the later legislation to prohibit the Postal Service from calling a magazine a letter at whim. Steve Kelly stated the concern of the MPA on this problem of allowing the Postal Service to interpret these statutes arbitrarily. If that continued:

> . . . the option of alternate delivery by private means would exist at the discretion of the Postal Service and not as a matter of right subject to change only by the Congress. This would inhibit the development of alternate delivery systems in the private sector; for any time a feasible and economical private system were developed that diverted newspapers and periodicals from the Postal Service, the suspension could be revoked administratively and the prospective increased volume necessary to the success of private delivery would be effectively cut off.

As for the legitimacy of the postal monopoly, the case for abolishing the Private Express Statutes is a standard libertarian argument. Robert Kephart, publisher of *Human Events,* has stated: "I do not agree in theory with the concept of government subsidy through non-compensatory postal rates of magazines and publications. I would vastly prefer to see postal services demonopolized; and the rise of a free market competition in delivery of all classes of mail. . . ."

This view has gained increasing support and respectability through the publication of a monograph by John Haldi, "Postal Monopoly, An Assessment of the Private Express Statutes" (Washington: The American Institute for Public Policy Research, February 1974). Mr. Haldi is an economic consultant who helped establish the Office of Planning in the Post Office. His message is succinct: ". . . it is pointed out that the statutory postal monopoly has no economic justification. The monopoly is no longer an important source of governmental revenue and in no way promotes better or cheaper mail service. In fact, it probably impedes the development of better systems for delivering written communications."

Part of Haldi's argument revolves around the proposition that the Postal Service monopoly is simply too large, that the economies of scale have been surpassed. If part of the postal mail volume could be handled by private competitors, the efficiency of the Postal Service in handling the rest would rise. His most telling argument is implicit in the question Why, if the Postal Service constitutes a "natural monopoly," does it require statutory protection?

Two similar bills have been introduced in Congress, in fact, to test this assertion. Both would abolish the Private Express Statutes, thus ending the postal monopoly over first-class mail, third-class addressed mail, and the monopoly use of your mailbox.

The most compelling feature of Representative Philip Crane's (R. Ill.) argument is that there is literally nothing to lose, as far as the taxpayers are concerned, in abolishing the postal monopoly. Some claim, for example, that competition would mean higher costs. According to Crane, however:

> Private businessmen know that an inability to produce for less cost would mean no realistic competition even if it were legal to compete. The fact is that the government-controlled post

154

office would be in jeopardy only if it is inefficient and only if competitors could perform for less costs. Thus, the public has nothing to lose from removing the Private Express Statutes and a great deal to gain.

A survey by McKinsey and Company, Crane claims, shows that the private delivery of local mail would cut costs to the users by 43 percent and yield a profit of 18 percent on investment to the firm delivering the mail.

The Postal Service and the postal unions, as one might anticipate, are vigorously opposed to opening up first-class mail to competition. In March 1974 Assistant Postmaster General Ralph Nicholson stated that "from the point of view of the whole public and not from the point of view of some specialized segment of the public, I believe Mr. Crane's proposal would be disastrous or near disastrous, both in terms of higher costs for the public and in terms of the quality of the service."

James Rademacher, also arguing against Crane's view, stressed the trust that the public places on the letter carrier, and the dark implications of privately hired carriers approaching the sacrosanct mailbox. "The letter carrier is charged with the security and sanctity of the United States mails. People entrust everything to the care of their mailmen. . . ." Mr. Rademacher also insisted that the price of a first-class letter was the "biggest bargain in the world today," even though he acknowledged to Crane that the price will soon be fifteen cents—thanks to his union's demands.

CORRUPTION

Over the years, the abuse of power has rampaged like a virus through the postal system. It has taken many shapes, from the direct payoff for favorable legislation, to silencing employees and delaying congressional hearings, to more subtle forms of corruption, including self-indulgence, nepotism, cronyism, and the awarding of contracts on a noncompetitive basis.

A good deal of opportunity for the payoff existed around postal rates when they were decided by the Congress. Congress was under constant pressure to come up with legislation to help out a needy publisher, religious group, or mail-order business. Such favors tended to be mutual, and how much money has gone under the table will never be known. Former Senator Daniel Brewster (D., Md.), for example, was convicted in 1972 for accepting a bribe from Speigel, Inc., a Chicago mail-order house. Brewster charged that he was innocent, but that thirty other members of Congress, "some of the most respected men in Congress," had accepted contributions from Speigel. Although the incident seems strangely old-fashioned nowadays, Brewster was convicted of accepting money from a lobbyist, in return for favorable votes on postal legislation. (His conviction was overturned, however, in 1974.)

True to tradition, the new Postal Service has occasionally proved vulnerable to charges of postal wrongdoing. For example, in May 1971 Westinghouse received a Postal Service contract for $3,465,753 for a job evaluation program, even though it had little experience in the field and had submitted the highest bid. A congressional subcommittee investigation at first concluded that strange as the circumstances were, there was really nothing amiss. The Hanley subcommittee report in April 1974, however, advised the Postal Service to declare the contract null and void, to try to recover the money and to improve its bidding award procedures.

In March 1973, during the House and Senate hearings on postal performance, Representative Charles H. Wilson said he was "shocked" to learn that former Postmaster Blount had been given an $18 million contract to build a bulk-mail processing plant at Des Moines, Iowa. Wilson charged that because of his former position, Blount had an unfair bidding advantage. Nonetheless, Blount's bid was low and he got the job. From then on anyone with the name of Blount was suspect in Wilson's book. He next brought up an allegation of wrongdoing concerning a Bobby Blount of San Diego who had received contracts from the Postal Service, rising from $15,000 to $96,000, allegedly because of his association with the Blounts of Postal Service fame. Klassen investigated this and vigorously denied any family connection. Bobby Blount said that his name similarity had probably hurt him more than it had helped, and that he had received the additional business because his bid was about one-third lower than the closest competitor.

The Jack Anderson charges on postal extravagance mentioned earlier were supplemented by Les Gapay, of *The Wall Street Journal*, in August 1973, with tales of cronyism in contracts for public relations service. The cronyism rumors in the Post Office have regularly centered about the number of former American Can people now in the Postal Service. On August 14, 1973, in an interview with Klassen, I asked him about those allegations. He responded with a professional "I'm glad you asked that," went on to say that there really weren't many of his ex-colleagues in the new Post Office, then turned the question. "How would you handle a new job? Wouldn't you get people you knew and trusted who were capable?"

According to Gapay, Mr. Klassen authorized $821,845 in noncompetitive public relations contracts over a three-year period to Bunaford & Company, headed by an old friend, Charles Bunaford. This amounted to about one fourth of the firm's revenue during the period. At first the Postal Service spokesmen denied the contracts existed, and then, like the San Clemente house repairs, they came to light and grew larger. As Postmaster General, Klassen had, in fact, authorized $404,655; the balance, which postal representatives had conveniently overlooked, was while Klassen was Deputy Postmaster General. In all there were twelve contracts.

One of the largest of these was for $343,000 to explain the Postal Service to its own employees (amazingly, only 11 percent knew of the change by March 1973) and to the public, which probably had an even lower awareness level. Some $33,974 was spent for the Washington Conference in February 1973 between Klassen and the eighty-five district managers, lauded by Senator Moss, followed by an $83,857 contract to handle management conferences on regional levels. The Postal Service has, in fact, a communications department of sixty-eight employees with a budget of $2.3 million, but this is not one of Mr. Klassen's favorite departments. He once referred to it as consisting of "sixteen shoe clerks," a phrase coined by Mr. Bunaford as part of his quest for postal contracts. Indeed, Bunaford's handling of public relations was far from the shoe store approach. The "presidential corridor" in a swank hotel at $550 per night was booked for a conference in San Fransico to billet Mr. Klassen and four other postal executives.

Another event causing raised eyebrows was the July 1973 conference in the Sheraton-Silver Spring Hotel in a Washington suburb where 250 postal managers sat in groups to exchange ideas, air their complaints, and propose ways that Headquarters could better perform its functions. The meeting started on a Wednesday night and lasted through "tough, long sessions all day Thursday and Friday," according to the Postal Service. This was an occasion for the top management to meet the next echelon and talk things over. "The session in which top management responded to suggestions and recommendations was sent back to Headquarters via a telephone line and broadcast over loudspeakers there. The program was taped and immediately rebroadcast for those who couldn't hear it the first time." Besides, the conference rooms did "double duty" for meetings of other groups and briefings by the various assistant postmasters general. Some thought room could have been found for this meeting in the massive Postal Service headquarters just ten miles away.

In April 1974 Jack Anderson again rattled the postal cage, this time claiming that the Postal Service was "plagued by problems," caused by poor management and collusion with contractors. Anderson contended that since

1971, about half of all postal contracts had been awarded on a noncompetitive basis. He also accused the Postal Service of wasting millions of dollars on outmoded machines to mechanize the mail, and of a $60 million cost overrun on the bulk-mail plant at Secaucus, New Jersey.

Postmaster General Klassen denounced Anderson, saying that his article "contains so many wrong conclusions that I feel compelled to respond." He thereupon showed that 24.8 percent of Postal Service contracts were sole source, or noncompetitive, but that each one had been justified. Experimentation with new machinery was part of the service's ongoing program and the bulk-mail plants were on budget. In concluding, he again addressed the matter of contracts. "What Mr. Anderson has done is to take a number of contracts and through innuendo, half-truth and misinformation, use them to imply mismanagement by the Board of Governors and the present management." Nonetheless, the Postal Service now issues a twice-monthly report, listing all contracts in excess of $5,000 and stating which were competitive and which were sole source.

In June 1974 Anderson was back on the job, accusing Klassen of accepting $20,000 in fees from a firm doing business with the Postal Service. Klassen acknowledged accepting the money, but his legal counsel, Louis Cox, said there was no conflict of interest or illegality involved.

These periodic exposés were useful in trying to make the public aware of what the giant Postal Service was doing, even though secrecy of operation of the Postal Service was and is the order of the day. It reminded Klassen, however, that a government corporation is as vulnerable to charges of impropriety as anyone else. The Bunaford connection was quietly terminated. A number of congressional members, including Morris K. Udall, had called for Klassen's resignation, although the problems of the post office extend beyond the performance of one man.

The actual use of postal funds for indoctrination conferences, however, is a different matter. This was a management decision, and one within the prerogative of the Postal Service. The corruptive aspect here is that dedication is interpreted as allegiance to the Postal Service and its leaders rather than to public service. Given the Postal Service's authority and its determination to ape the ways of big business, it is important that restraints be built into the system, such as legislation requiring competitive bids, close auditing by the General Accounting Office, and consumer or public members of the Board of Governors to issue independent reports on the Postal Service's performance.

According to the Postal Service, the above rash of management meetings gave a real boost to the postal family. This leads one to wonder why they weren't initiated sooner. Klassen himself said, speaking of the February 1973 powwow: "Most of these men [district managers] were 50 years old and had 25 years of experience. They were divided into groups of 8 or 9 with one leader. They were told to make their recommendations freely. Forget whose toes you might be stepping on."

The focus of these meetings was to instill a sense of responsibility and initiative in men who had for years taken orders from Washington. Klassen also worked to improve service morale. Special stamps and "Postal Week" were initiated to honor postal workers and customers. "By

161

law, your Postal Service–and the men and women who operate it–is obligated to serve your community and the nation on a non-profit basis, with courtesy and care, and to keep postal costs in balance with postal revenue," intoned Klassen. "To do this, the mail service needs the informed understanding, cooperation, support and constructive suggestions of every citizen and community." Other morale boosters include the yearly Outstanding Handicapped Postal Employee Awards competition. (More than 22,000 postal workers are handicapped, making the Postal Service one of the nation's largest employees of this group.)

The emphasis on better wages, morale, and working conditions has met with a strong response in terms of job applications. Between January 1973, which marked the ending of the postal manpower freeze, and May of that year, over 130,000 formal applications were filed. About 100,000 passed the examinations. Former Assistant Postmaster General for Public Relations William Eudey said that "over the past few years the relative economic standing of Postal Service jobs has changed significantly." On the pre-July 1973 labor settlement base, employees after eight years would rise to $11,073, with federal retirement, vacation, and paid holidays, all particularly attractive, said Mr. Eudey. "In years past, Postal Service jobs were attractive primarily for their security. . . . But things are different today in the new-styled Postal Service, which is no longer under political patronage control. Pay has moved up to comparability with private industry. . . [and] people see their new Postal Service in a new light–one that spells out not just security, but new career and financial opportunities too."

In light of its new philosophy, the Postal Service could not help but be pleased with its July 1973 labor agreement. The new contract allowed the postal managers to "run the business," according to Darrell F. Brown, Senior Assistant Postmaster General for Employee and Labor Relations, and longtime associate of Klassen in industrial relations at American Can. The agreement was signed with the four AFL-CIO unions: the American Postal Workers Union; the National Association of Letter Carriers; the National Post Office Mail Handlers, Watchmen, Messengers and Group Leaders Division of the Laborers' International Union of North America; and the National Rural Letter Carriers Association. Under its terms, any possibility of wildcat strikes, which would have rekindled public and congressional concern over the capability of the postal leadership as custodians of the mails, was averted.

Not everyone shared Klassen's position that the labor settlement was a good one, or joined in the jubilation of the postal unions. According to *Business Week* in its June 23, 1973, issue, "The United States Postal Service, in its eagerness to avoid another showdown with its militant unions, has set a dangerous precedent for wage negotiations between the federal government and its employees. The quasi-government corporation has agreed to a two-year wage increase of 14 percent, and on top of that it has consented to unlimited cost-of-living adjustments during the life of the contract."

Business Week believed that this agreement cut out the ground from under private employers who had been resisting unlimited cost-of-living increases. Since the wage raise was not related to increased productivity, it was, in effect, a bonus in *Business Week*'s view, something due to labor regardless of performance. Performance being notoriously bad, "why this performance record should be rewarded with a wage raise is beyond explanation." Instead of taking advantage of this initial bargaining under the government corporation to set up wage guidelines based on productivity increases, the contract was "clearly inflationary," *Business Week* continued, and the Postal Service would pass along the cost to its "captive customers through another increase in mail charges."

Darrell Brown assessed the matter differently. He felt the contract language was "more clear, more complete and more precise" than in the 1971 agreement and added: "it comes closer to being the kind of agreement that has proven to be workable in the private sector. And it challenges postal managers to manage the business according to the postal philosophy." This philosophy, Brown elaborated, was a humane program of delivering letters fast and economically.

Where the current labor policy will lead remains an open question. One thing is certain, however. It will surely result in higher postal rates. For their part, the unions are content. In the midst of press and congressional clamor for Klassen to resign in October 1974, the headline of Mike Causey's column read, "Postal Unions Want Klassen to Stay." Small wonder.

XII

TOWARD A NEW POSTAL POLICY

Early in 1974 I asked Senator Fong if he could describe, in one sentence, the single most serious deficiency in the Postal Service. "The main problem," he answered quickly, "is that the Postmaster General does not have his own money invested in it."

The Postal Service is not a private business, nor is it a public business. It is everybody's business and nobody's business. This leaves in limbo the key issues of just how the mails should be delivered, and who is to pay for what. The answers to these questions cannot long be postponed. Given the whopping 1974 postal deficit, it is clear that if economy of operations was the goal of the Kappel Commission in establishing the postal corporation it has totally failed in its aim. It is equally apparent that the Postal Service cannot endure in its present form.

It is time to take a fresh, imaginative look at our postal operations in terms of public policy. Whatever organizational form postal delivery takes, the customer must come first. The business life of the country, as well as many of our cultural and educational benefits, are hostage to the mails.

Each additional month that postal-related issues remain unresolved the more traumatic their necessary, inevitable, and final resolution will be. As taxpayers, we have a tremendous stake in the proper sorting out of the mails, both in terms of our pocketbooks and in terms of the service we receive. It is imperative that we face up to the present postal crisis and determine which way to go from here.

By July 1975 the Postal Service will have been in operation as a government corporation for four years. The current management has learned a great deal about the politics of the postal business and has lain the groundwork for a more highly mechanized (but questionable) sorting and movement of the mails. It has been wasteful and profligate in its spending. The 1973 hearings were a kind of mass congressional catharsis, purging legislators of their guilt and frustration at having abandoned their responsibilities to their constituents as effective watchdogs of the mails. As much as it would like to forget the Postal Service, Congress has been forced to reenter the picture because of the failure of the reorganization. With each month that the Postal Service functions as a government corporation, it becomes harder for Congress to handle, without new legislation.

The new postal bureaucracy has grown in strength like a coral reef. Even a series of pieces in the Washington *Post* in June 1974 by Ronald Kessler, entitled "The Great Mail Bungle," failed to stir real action or dent the Postal Service's facade. Any other institution in Washington, save the

Pentagon, would have crumbled under Kessler's barrage of damaging evidence on rates, delivery performance, and mismanagement. The Postal Service was aided in its escape by scattered elements in Congress who are reluctant to come to grips with the problem, as well as by a nagging suspicion in some quarters that the whole muddle may be unsolvable. The special-interest groups, moreover, from advertising mailers to postal unions, are in conflict over the best solution.

The lack of congressional wisdom in turning over $4 billion of public assets for the benefit of postal management and its employees under the guise of better and cheaper service is now obvious to all. Like General Motors, the Postal Service is serving the public in a sense; but overwhelmingly, like other corporations large and small, it operates in its own best interests. Mr. Kappel has expressed the thought that the performance of the Postal Service might inspire the government to convert other public assets into government corporations. What might be next? The Park Service? The Department of Commerce? If in the case of the Postal Service, the change to a government corporation had indeed been successful, a useful precedent would have been established. But the performance of the Postal Service has shown only the failings of the government corporation idea. True, the actual service is not likely to get much worse; the real bomb in the mailbag is runaway costs.

Two obvious ways of reducing postal delivery costs have not even been tried. The first is to further reduce delivery, especially Saturday delivery, a position advocated by the Associated Third-Class Mail Users and opposed by the postal unions. A second method would be to standardize the size of envelopes, perhaps settling on two or three sizes. This would allow postal sorting machines of a cheaper variety to work effectively. Here the hang-up seems to be within the Postal Service itself, based on the same logic that allows fireworks to be sold on the Fourth of July for fear of interfering with a citizen's right to self-mutilation. A low rate could be established for standardized, machine-sorted envelopes and a much higher rate for hand-sorted letters. These two measures alone might turn around the economics of the Postal Service. The fact that neither are being attempted or even seriously planned gives the coup de grâce to the myth of the Postal Service's "businesslike" approach.

It is all too clear that creating a government corporation did not improve postal service at lower costs. The critics of postal reorganization cited earlier now appear to have been prophets. To believe that there is something inherent in government ownership, semi-public ownership, or private ownership that has relevance to the real problem and purpose of postal service—delivery of the best service at the lowest price—is to confuse ownership with marketing. By claiming that the problem with the old Post Office was "politics," the reorganization focused on the wrong issue. Under the government corporation, we are saddled with a band of like-minded men licensed to impose their will on the nation's mail service. All in the line of duty they have raised top salaries and headquarters administrative costs to shocking heights and come to a sweetheart agreement with the four postal unions that has had disastrous effects not only on the Postal Service itself but on the whole federal bureaucracy.

The thesis that rational methods of doing business are only found outside the structure of government has yet to be proven by the Postal Service. The ineptitude demonstrated by Postal Service management, be it in terms of chauffeured cars or "noncompetitive" contracts, should suffice to show that if we really want a less expensive Department of Defense, for example, the answer is not a government corporation.

Where, then, does the solution to our postal problems lie?

A new postal policy might call for changes within the existing structure (the patchwork theory) with special emphasis on improving the Postal Service management and increasing its responsiveness to public control. Or it might dictate a return to the old system, ending the charade of a business-oriented company and reestablishing the concept of public service and public financing. A third approach might be to open the system to private competition across the board, in the process determining just what elements of postal communications are essential rather than simply acquiescing to the electronic message-moving revolution.

Yet another possible direction would be to reconsider the whole idea of mechanization. Perhaps utilizing more employees (at lower pay scale) and fewer machines might be a good way to cope with the foreseeable rise in unemployment in this and following decades brought in by market saturation and the decline in the requirement for workers. In a sense, the Postal Service program was conceived by men who were trying to eliminate jobs while the current national requirement in terms of social policy is to find areas that could be labor intensive.

A word about the general competitive position of the

Postal Service in today's market is in order here. As fiscal year 1974 demonstrated, the Postal Service's economic position is deteriorating. Major competition for postal business is coming from other directions than the UPS or local private delivery systems in terms of the 90 billion mail volume of 1975. As pointed out in the Kappel report, 40 percent of the mail is "transaction" mail. Each time the first class stamp goes up two cents (which will happen with regularity under the present organization, unless multibillion-dollar subsidies are instigated), it becomes more feasible for competing electronic systems to move a substantial part of the business mail. Take, for example, personal checking payment of such items as utility bills and mortgages. With proper coding, perhaps developing around an individual's social security number, a single central tape operating through the "full-service banks" could take off these deductions each month as well as adding on paychecks. Along these lines, in the fall of 1973, the Federal Reserve Board in conjunction with the Air Force paid twenty thousand airmen, who volunteered to participate, their salaries by magnetic tape. The tape was sent to a district Federal Reserve Bank, which in turn electronically sorted the paycheck information and delivered it to the twelve Federal Reserve districts which in turn forwarded the information to individual commercial banks where the personnel had their accounts. The test was aimed at reducing the cost of making payments and cutting down on the river of checks. It was successful and is being continued.

At the moment 27 billion paper checks are written annually, and at this rate, by 1985, the number will rise to 60 billion. The cost of processing a single check through the banking system is now eighteen cents. The cost of the magnetic tape system is less than a penny. The Federal Reserve Board hopes that eventually almost all banking can be done electronically, with even individual families making electronic payments and deposits from their homes. As the monthly charges for checking accounts necessarily rise, so will the volume of electronic banking.

With each stride forward in technology, the Postal Service will become increasingly vulnerable to competitive methods of message moving. The new Xerox facsimile system, for example, is moving information over the phone at a rapidly growing rate. Microwave circuits are loaded and AT&T's new ninety-six-city network for transmitting digital information will be in operation in 1976. The Postal Service is aware of existing plans in the electronic field and keeps up to date through the office of the assistant postmaster general for planning.

Electronic transmissions are, according to J. T. Ellington, Jr., former assistant postmaster general for planning, the number-one threat to the Postal Service. Of the 300 billion messages sent in the United States yearly, about 170 billion are by telephone and telegraph and about 90 billion by the Postal Service. Checkless banking will eat into postal volume, as the Federal Reserve program mentioned above gets under way. Cable television may allow print-out of materials by the home receiver, furthering cutting into postal business. The Postal Service itself is working on wider use of facsimile transmission to meet this kind of competition and public resistance to postal rate hikes.

Returning to the question of postal reform, there is general agreement that it is imperative that appropriate

171

control over our vast mail system be restored to the citizen and Congress so that decisions with necessarily long lead times to important goals can be dispassionately reviewed. If the Postal Service is to be continued, this can only be done through the reorganization of the Board of Governors. (If the board is not reorganized, it may be eliminated altogether, as proposed by Representative Charles Wilson in May 1974, its authority and accountability going to the Postmaster General, who would be appointed by the President with the advice and consent of the Senate.)

As we have seen, there are two main deficiences in the board as now constructed. First, a serious lack of experience among board members in postal affairs, due to an overzealous attempt to avoid "special interests," and second, the fact that all the directors are from business or utility backgrounds. In many corporations, large and small, it makes little difference who the directors are, since corporate policy is actually determined by one person or a like-minded group and the board is little more than gild on the lily. (Anyone who has served on a private school board or small private company board where his only function was to meet the laws of incorporation is familiar with this fact of life.) In the case of the Postal Service, however, the composition of the board *is* important since it is in a position to make decisions and offer advice on the running of the gigantic Postal Service. Responsible only to the President of the United States—as noted earlier, former Board Chairman Kappel did not see the President officially *for over five years*—the board enjoys almost total autonomy. The public and the Congress are deliberately kept very much in the dark concerning the decision-making process as the following board meeting report, quoted here in full, demonstrates:

> I hereby certify that the following is a true and accurate excerpt from the minutes of a meeting of the Board of Governors of the United States Postal Service held on April 6, 1971:
>
> Mr. Hargrove was then asked to outline the various ways in which the first issue of Postal Service bonds might be marketed. After discussion, and upon motion duly made, second and carried (Mr. Braun not participating), the management was authorized to commence negotiations for the underwriting of an issue of bonds by the Postal Service in the amount of $250 million.

The problems posed by the board's inexperience in postal matters and its biased outlook are compounded by the lack of effective government control over board matters. The President of the United States understandably has other things on his mind! Taking the Postal Service out of the realm of politics is one thing but removing a public corporation from public control and responsibility is another. The Postal Service has succeeded so far in avoiding the sounding of the general alarm only because the public is generally unaware of the deficiencies and lack of supervision surrounding management, attributing poor postal service to a series of quirks and blunders. However, as mismanagement becomes increasingly apparent in the form of the annual rise in postal costs, the scales will finally fall from the public's eyes.

The congressional hearings in 1973 raised the question of the composition of the Board of Governors, with Representative Udall stating that he had hoped that the Postmaster would want one or more retired postal officials on the board so that they could leaven the formless mass of members with their experience. The resistance to this idea under Blount continued under Kappel. Management shows a dogged refusal to learn from the past.

To effect postal reform under the patchwork theory of salvaging the Postal Reorganization Act, it would be necessary through legislation to place three members selected by Congress on the board. The presidential appointees would outnumber those of the Congress eight to three; thus in terms of votes the latter group would be relatively insignificant. But its very presence would keep the board on its toes in terms of public responsibility. With the congressionally appointed members assuring the prompt release of appropriate information to Congress and the public, the reign of Postal Service secrecy would come to an end. The congressional members would also be entitled to a small staff to keep them informed of Postal Service operations, supplementing the work of the Government Accounting Office.

Successful application of the patchwork theory to the Postal Service's labor problems would have to begin at the top. Headquarters could easily be reduced by half, and the number of overpaid bureaucrats reduced still further. There are 109 jobs in the Postal Service with salary levels authorized at over $40,000, and here as elsewhere in the government, high salaries eliminate competition and the exigencies of the balance sheet as motives for hard-driving top performance. A gentle upward creeping of personnel into the higher grades, evident throughout the federal bureaucracy, helps explain why the budget for the civil service and Postal Service rises ever upward, while the number of workers holds steady or even drops, especially in the lower levels of the Postal Service.

In the *Congressional Record* of February 26, 1973, Representative H. R. Gross reiterated his opposition to Mr. Kappel's position that the $60,000 maximum pay should be increased for the Postal Service. Commented Gross: "The material I received fails to convince me that the salary range of postal executives is not attractive, and I see little, if any, evidence that the present incumbents of these fancy-salaried jobs made any financial sacrifice in accepting employment with the Postal Service."

The record fiscal 1974 deficit blew the whistle on the myth that things were getting better at the Postal Service. More hearings were called in February 1975 to ponder the tea leaves. Many left the halls of Congress thinking the unthinkable: The ship was going to sink.

The Penn Central case may be all too pertinent to the final outcome of the postal reorganization. Few among us would have guessed ten years ago that the Penn Central, the country's most prestigious railroad, a big board company, paying four-dollar dividends religiously, would be bankrupt by 1970. Its overpaid, myopic management watched the organization go down the drain, apparently only realizing toward the end that it was time to sell their stock, take their pensions, and get out fast. Many will be tried in courts of law.

The collapse of the once-proud Rolls-Royce Ltd., due to

a single management blunder in underbidding on the RB-211 engine for Lockheed, is another in the recent series of corporate horror shows. The official British Government report contains this interchange between a member of the board of inquiry and Mr. R. Nicholson, manager of the RB-211 project.

> Q. If you were asked to say in a sentence what went wrong, which I dare say you have been asked to say a hundred times by different people in the last year, what does it come to? Can it be put in a sentence? Does it simply mean: We failed to appreciate it was going to cost us so much?
>
> A. Yes.
>
> Q. You would probably not much like to put it in a sentence?
>
> A. I cannot improve upon that. It sounds a very crude way of putting it, but I cannot improve upon it. We did not know. We ought to have known, there is no question. We just have to look at the history of projects through the nineteen sixties, and I blame myself and I blame the remainder of the directors, and particularly, the non-executive directors of the company for not asking that very simple question.
>
> Q. Had you allowed enough for contingencies?
>
> A. It was not asked.

Are the fates of the Penn Central and Rolls-Royce a foreshadowing of the end of the Postal Reorganization Act of 1970? The factors are all there—a small, secretive board of directors, bemused management, doubtful investment decisions, increasingly noncompetitive operations, and skyrocketing labor costs with a no-layoff clause in the labor contract.

It is certain that the no-layoff clause settled upon in the July 1973 two-year labor agreement is extremely damaging to the flexibility and efficiency of Postal Service operations. If the unions continue to win this point, excess labor costs that have long plagued the railroads will be permanently built into the Postal Service. A no-layoff policy also seems inconsistent with efforts to mechanize the system.

An additional labor issue that merits close scrutiny in terms of the future of the mails is the right to strike. Postmaster General Klassen did not oppose this principle in the March 1973 hearings, providing that the bargaining was between the unions and the Postal Service, without Congress as the middleman. He later, however, recommended to the Board of Governors that the Postal Service oppose the measure, which it successfully did. There are proposals in Congress, nevertheless, for right-to-strike legislation, including one introduced by Jerome R. Waldie (D., Calif.) in February 1973. According to Waldie, without the right to strike, the postal unions are a "paper dragon," and are reduced to a kind of "collective begging."

In a sense, of course, the right-to-strike issue is rhetorical, since, as George Meany pointed out, if the deal's not right, there will be strikes anyway, by a different name to avoid violating the law. This was effectively demonstrated by the wildcat strikes or job actions in March 1970, which resulted in the National Guard sorting out the mail.

177

A legal position allowing strikes would strengthen the union's hands. The Postal Service management, under constant pressure from right-to-strike lobbies, is strongly inclined to reach any agreement, any kind of settlement, to avoid a work stoppage which with its ensuing havoc would move Congress back into the center of the postal scene. Further, a strike of any kind would emphasize again the nation's vulnerability to the postal unions. This in turn would lead to more clamor for repeal of the Private Express Statutes, for only real competition would insure the public of reliable alternate service.

In certain aspects of its labor policy, the Postal Service does in fact seem to be speeding the day of its personal Penn Central crisis. As Mike Causey, of the Washington *Post,* noted in his column of August 11, 1973, "Postal Unit Is Leader in Fringes":

> Postal employees, among the most unionized workers in government, have pulled well ahead of their white collar civil service counterparts in money-in-the-bank fringe benefits. As usual, 1.2 million white collar, VA medical and Foreign Service personnel find themselves in the position of trying to catch up to, or match, benefits already won by the muscle of 600,000 organized postals.

This is the kind of competition that brings little joy to the soul of the taxpayer or consumer of postal and government services. Also in the patchwork theory, Congress should be required to approve the final labor contract to be certain it does not throw out of kilter the whole federal pay system.

In the job of moving the mails, two obvious steps could be taken that would be of benefit to the taxpayer. First, more use should be made of Amtrak. Both the Postal Service and Amtrak are government corporations, and both are heavily subsidized. It would seem to make sense to move more mail between cities by the passenger trains, even if it might take longer, assuming the mail was low priority and the standard of delivery was well understood. It would also seem sensible to use the military air transportation system to move as much mail as possible. Many still remember the heroism of the Army in the 1930s trying to fly open biplanes through hail and sleet, until too many crashes brought an early end to the experiment. But nowadays, instead of training flights, why not use the giant transports and the $10,000 a year second lieutenants to help out with the mail? Instead, the costly planes and pilots are idle, while the Postal Service duplicates what those assets could accomplish through expensive private contracts. The mixture of public and private interests in our transportation and communications systems is curious to begin with, and the lack of rational utilization of national investments is a source of wonder.

The Postal Service has a strong, energetic facade and a fast line of chatter. Under the present management, however, it is busily becoming a classic white elephant with its large investment in unneeded buildings and inappropriate machines, indissoluble, expensive labor force, and vast, top-management bureaucracy. Its chances of survival in its present form are zero.

The acceleration of postal rates and costs has again called into question the basic ideas behind the Postal Reorganization Act, whether Congress does not, in fact, have a responsibility to insure the proper operation of the mails and whether in the public interest the "break-even" philosophy might not be abandoned. Representative Hanley's new 20 percent subsidy measure was, by his own admission, designed in part to "create a national debate on how the government should approach the costs of the Postal Service."

From the point of view of the Postal Service professionals, a return to the congressional subsidy as proposed by Representative Hanley would be the end of the road. But there are many supporters of such a move. Former Postmaster General Day, for example, thinks subsidy in regard to the movement of the mail is the wrong term altogether. In commenting on Kappel's opposition to Hanley's proposal, Day said, "But would he feel that the businessman who goes to the Department of Commerce for advice or information is being subsidized because the Department does not make him pay a fee? Of course not. Mr. Kappel would readily recognize that service from the Department of Commerce is something he pays for with his tax money and is entitled to get as a tax payer. A man who takes his family to Yellowstone National Park is certainly not being 'subsidized' merely because the entrance fee he pays is small in relation to what it costs the Government to make the facilities available." Day concluded that this kind of talk of Kappel's on the mail subsidy was "simplistic" and was based "upon the unproven and unprovable assumption that the taxpayer is entitled to nothing whatever for his tax money where the Post Office is concerned, but is entitled to all kinds of free services—very often much less essential—from other Federal Agencies. The Post Office furnishes a service which practically everyone wants and uses and is glad to have."

As we have seen, the attitude of former Postmaster General Klassen toward subsidies changed dramatically in the spring of 1974. It is becoming increasingly apparent to top Postal Service management that only a large and permanent public subsidy of the magnitude Representative Hanley has suggested will prevent postal rates from going so high that the hue and cry from the public will bring about "major changes," i.e., threaten established management's control of the Postal Service.

In fiscal 1976 the postal budget will exceed $12 billion. Based on Hanley's 20 percent formula, should it become law, the Treasury's contribution would be $2.4 billion and rising. It is against this background that the idea of breaking the postal monopoly will come into sharp focus. John Haldi states in his abovementioned study that "neither the long history of postal monopoly nor concern for the current beneficiaries of its implicit taxation should stay Congress from setting the situation right. Mail communications are too important to be left to the mercy of a large and unresponsive monopolist." Will he prove to be prophetic?

Whatever course Congress takes, massive subsidy or private competition, the Postal Service as envisioned by the Postal Reorganization Act is dead. Architects of future postal policy might do well to reflect upon the message engraved on New York City's main post office building:

181

Not snow, nor rain, nor heat nor gloom of night stays these couriers from the swift completion of their appointed rounds.

It is time that the spirit of public service prevail again in the mails.